Our Neighbours' Voices Will We Listen?

The Interfaith Social Assistance Reform Coalition

An Our Schools/Our Selves Series Title

James Lorimer & Company Ltd., Publishers
Toronto, 1998

James Lorimer & Company Ltd. acknowledges the support of the Department of Canadian Heritage and the Ontario Arts Council in the development of writing and publishing in Canada. We acknowledge the support of the Canada Council for the Arts for our publishing program.

Canadian Cataloguing in Publication Data

Interfaith Social Assistance Reform Coalition
Our neighbours' voices: will we listen?

(Our schools, our selves)
Including bibliographical references.
ISBN 1-55028-646-3

1. Poor — Ontario — Social conditions. 2. Poverty — Government policy — Ontario. 3. Public welfare — Ontario. I. Title. II. Series.

HC120.P6157 1998   362.5'09713   C98-932477-X

Design and typesetting: Nancy Reid
Cover Design: Nancy Reid
Photos: Vincenzo Pietropaolo

James Lorimer & Company Ltd., Publishers
35 Britain Street
Toronto M5A 1R7

Printed and bound in Canada

Contents

Our Neighbours' Voices

The Interfaith Social Assistance Reform Coalition (ISARC) is made up of many different faith communities in Ontario. Current members of the Coalition include representatives from (in alphabetical order):

Anglican Church of Canada
Baptist Convention of Ontario and Quebec
Buddhist Community of Greater Toronto
Canadian Council for Reform Judaism
Canadian Religious Conference, Ontario Region (Catholic Orders)
Christian Reformed Church
Canadian Unitarian Peace Fellowship
Citizens for Public Justice
Evangelical Lutheran Church in Canada, Eastern Synod
Islamic Foundation of Greater Toronto
Mennonite Central Committee, Ontario
Ontario Conference of Catholic Bishops
Presbyterian Church in Canada
Society of Friends (Quakers)
Toronto Board of Rabbis
United Church of Canada

Preface

Our Neighbours' Voices is dedicated to the many people who attended and spoke at Neighbour to Neighbour hearings throughout Ontario in 1997.

Many speakers were impoverished people who overcame their fears to reflect on their experiences and communicate their feelings. We have brought together their voices in this book to tell an important story about what is happening to poor and disenfranchised people in this province.

An important part of recognizing the human dignity of each person is to listen and let the person know that he or she is heard. The stories in this book are about real life experiences. We want people all across Ontario to listen and to find ways of letting lower-income people in their communities know that their stories have been heard. This is best done in community with our neighbours—rich and poor, young and old, those who live beside us and those who live in another part of town or another region of the province.

The listening and working together may not be easy because gaps between us are growing. But we call each other to community—just as the Interfaith Social Assistance Reform Coalition is a community of faith groups working together to care for our neighbour and seek justice.

We hope that each of us can honour the courage of those who spoke at the hearings by breaking through our own fears and prejudices which keep us from being a community. We are all responsible for making a better world for ourselves, our children and our neighbours.

ISARC appreciates the important contributions that each of the thirteen coordinating committees for the Neighbour to Neighbour hearings made to this process and to this book. We wish to thank Joel Klassen for all his work in reviewing the commentary from hundreds of people across the province and putting it all together in a written manuscript. Andy Mitchell generously helped us out with graphical material to illustrate the text, and Cheryl Hamilton provided editing services. We also appreciate that ISARC members gave their time freely to attend the hearings and provide guidance through the publication process.

We are able to publish *Our Neighbours' Voices* because of the generosity of the Atkinson Foundation.

And now this book is in the hands of its readers. May it guide and strengthen you as we build community among all the people of Ontario.

Brice Balmer, Susan Eagle, Gabrielle Mandel and David Pfrimmer
The Editorial Team for *Our Neighbours' Voices*

CHAPTER 1

Introduction

I am a single mother of a two-year-old. I am educated and in a desperate search for work. I am on welfare and very grateful for what I am receiving. However, it is not enough to cover my bills or eat three healthy meals a day. In order to feed my daughter, I don't eat breakfast, I go to a women's drop-in centre for lunch and ration my supper.

Jacqueline

A Call to Social Action

With the publication of *Our Neighbours' Voices*, the religious communities that belong to and support the Interfaith Social Assistance Reform Coalition (ISARC) hope to engage the minds and hearts of Ontario's citizens.

ISARC's purpose in publishing this book is to bring to public attention what is happening in Ontario—not just what is *happening* to those who are impoverished and marginalized, but what is happening to all of us. Because we are all implicated in and affected by the spread and deepening of poverty, hunger and homelessness in this province.

If we fail to respond adequately to the suffering of our neighbours who are in need, we weaken our communities. We jeopardize the fabric of social relationships that make our communities whole, that make our communities good places to live, work and raise children, and grow old.

This book is filled with the personal accounts of impoverished people who came to community meetings across Ontario during 1997. ISARC sponsored these Neighbour to Neighbour hearings to listen to those members of our communities whose voices are too often unheard or ignored.

ISARC challenges all of us to read the personal accounts in this book, and hear the voices of desperation, anger and despair. These are the voices of our neighbours. They have a moral claim on us, as a society, to meet their basic needs. And we are failing them.

ISARC challenges all of us to hear these accounts—of people struggling to maintain their dignity, find work, feed and clothe themselves and their children, put a roof over their heads, and keep alive some hope of a better future.

Listen to this comment at one of the community hearings: "A lot of us feel like we're going through the Second Great Depression. And we're trying to survive. But the difference between this depression and the other is that there are lots of people out there who aren't hurting along with us. They're kind of leaving us behind and not caring."

But we must do more than listen. We must *respond*.

Traditionally, one response of religious communities and many people of good will has been charity. But charity is not the solution. Charity is an important response to urgent human needs, and faith communities, among others, have actively supported food banks, emergency shelters and other community efforts to help people in crisis.

But charity is no substitute for justice. A just and inclusive society enables people to take their rightful place in the community. Building such a society is both a religious and a public responsibility. Charitable actions can complement government efforts, but charity cannot and should not replace government's responsibility to safeguard and ensure the well-being of all members of our communities.

The Need for a Social Vision

Today, in Ontario, economic uncertainty and confrontational politics have eroded our sense of compassion. The prevailing sense of fear and insecurity that has afflicted us all has led to a willingness to believe the worst about each other, particularly the poor and the unemployed. We seem to have lost our social vision—our shared sense of the common good and our responsibilities to each other.

Our governments reflect this lack of social vision. Provincially, the government has implemented policies that penalize the poor and shift resources away from those most in need. The federal government has abandoned national standards and ignored international covenants that recognize our obligations to those in need.

ISARC believes that we must reclaim a vision of a just and inclusive society. We must demand that our governments accept their responsibility—on our behalf, because public policy is an expression of the collective will—to ensure that the basic material needs of all Ontarians are met and that all members of our society have the chance to escape a life of poverty.

We call on our fellow Ontarians to make a commitment to justice and to a new social vision for this province—a vision that is founded in the principles of human dignity, mutual responsibility, social equity, economic equity, fiscal fairness, and ecological sustainability.

There are recommendations in this book that strive to move us closer to this vision. We hope our fellow Ontarians will consider these recommendations, support them and work for their implementation. As one of the participants in the Neighbour to Neighbour hearings told us: "Everybody's using what I call the language of compliance—trying to keep people quiet and calm. They are not saying: Get up and get angry. Start doing."

The Principles of a New Social Vision

Human Dignity
The right of all persons and their communities to be treated with justice, love, compassion and respect, and their responsibility to treat others likewise.

Mutual Responsibility
The obligation of the community to care and share with its people, ensuring that basic needs are met.

Social Equity
The right of all people to adequate access to basic resources, to full participation in the life and decision-making of the community.

Economic Equity
The right of all persons and communities to adequate access to the resources necessary for a full life, including access to worthwhile work, fair employment considerations and income-security provisions, and our communal responsibility to use such resources responsibly.

Fiscal Fairness
The right of all persons, communities, and institutions to fair fiscal treatment and the responsibility of all to contribute fairly for the well-being of all.

Ecological Sustainability
The obligation of the community to practise responsible stewardship of the earth and its environment, so that creation might be preserved for generations to come.

As a community, we must ask ourselves: Are we content that our neighbour's children should go hungry, as long as our own children are well fed? Are we content to close our doors against the cold, as growing numbers of people with mental disabilities and other problems live on our streets? Are we so well protected against the whims of the world economy that we cannot imagine ever needing a sustaining hand at a time of need?

Giving some low-income people a chance to speak out in this book is not an end in itself. It is meant to galvanize all of us to respond to our neighbour.

ISARC's Mandate and Mission

The coalition of faith communities that forms ISARC was created in 1986. It was born out of hope—a hope that this group could contribute to the creation of new public policy that would bring greater justice and dignity for Ontarians marginalized by poverty.

In 1986, the Ontario government had appointed an independent Social Assistance Review Committee to consult, study and make recommendations on the future of the social assistance system (known commonly as welfare). The original mandate of ISARC was to provide advice to this Committee.

After two years of work, including a massive consultation process that generated more than 1,500 submissions, the Social Assistance Review Committee issued its landmark report, called *Transitions* (1988). It set out a detailed blueprint for a new welfare system, with the fundamental objective that "all people in Ontario are entitled to an equal assurance of life opportunities in a society that is based on fairness, shared responsibility, and personal dignity for all. The objective for social assistance therefore must be to ensure that individuals are able to make the transition from dependence to autonomy, and from exclusion on the margins of society to integration within the mainstream of community life."

Over the past decade, along with many other concerned groups, ISARC has advocated for implementation of the *Transitions* vision of an adequate, accessible, fair and accountable social assistance system. At the same time, our mandate has expanded beyond welfare to include the broader issues of poverty, hunger and homelessness. ISARC has met with political leaders from all parties, hosted hearings to give voice to low-income people, and made presentations whenever there was a platform available to us.

As the depth and pervasiveness of poverty have increased, as public attitudes have hardened, and as public policy responses have become less and less adequate, we have become increasingly alarmed.

ISARC has taken up this cause because of a simple message that is at the moral core of all the major faith traditions. It is a message of compassion and love for our neighbour and a call for justice to be done. To be a person of faith is to understand that each human being has a value and dignity that far transcends what society deems to be useful, practical, or affordable.

For Christians, we are to "... love your neighbour as yourself" (Matthew 22:24-40). For Jews, we are to "Do unto others as you would have them do unto you" (Leviticus 19:17). For Buddhists, we should "Hurt not others, in ways that you yourself would find hurtful" (Udana-Varga 5:18). In Islam, "No one of you is a believer until he desire for his brother that which he desires for himself" (Sumah).

This central teaching, shared among religious communities, is the moral imperative that inspires people of faith to respond to our neighbours in need.

To be a person of faith is to understand that each human being has a value and dignity that far transcends what society deems to be useful, practical, or affordable.

But how can we love our neighbour when there are thousands of neighbours in need? The answer is when justice is present. Justice is ensuring that we are in a right relationship with other people and within our communities. When there is hunger while some have too much to eat, or when there is homelessness while some live in luxury, or when there is poverty in the midst of affluence, justice is not present. Where justice is not present, the quality of human life and the humanity of our communities are degraded. This is not what faith compels us to work for in building our communities.

Justice is never done in the abstract, away from its consequences for the human community. Religious communities understand that the work of justice is never complete. But we expect our public institutions to be moving towards greater justice for those who are most vulnerable.

We are speaking out, through this publication, because we see governments and their public policies taking Ontario in the wrong direction. We believe it is up to people who who care about the future of our communities and our children to get us back on course.

Our hope is that this book will build greater understanding of what it means to be impoverished and how people end up in poverty. A volunteer at a soup kitchen commented: "What's missing in most of our lives is that we have not come face to face with a poor person."

The Neighbour to Neighbour Hearings

The testimonies in this book were gathered at Neighbour to Neighbours hearings during 1997 in Windsor, Owen Sound, London, Kitchener, St. Catharines, Hamilton, Toronto (three), Peterborough, Sudbury and Sault Ste. Marie. In addition, a series of parallel "People's Hearings" were held in the Ottawa area, resulting in a report called *People First, Les gens d'abord*.

The hearings were open to the public. Some took place in small and informal settings, others in larger centres, such as soup-kitchens. Local volunteer committees drawn from faith communities and other community groups organized each meeting. In some cases, in addition to listening, the group took time to discuss issues that were raised in the presentations. In most cases, a panel of local religious and community leaders had the responsibility of listening to the testimonies and summarizing their impressions of the day in writing.

This is actually the second time that ISARC has held Neighbour to Neighbour hearings. The first time was in 1990, two years after the release of *Transitions*, the report of the Social Assistance Review Committee. A report on those hearings, called *Neighbour to Neighbour: Voices for Change*, lamented the lack of progress in alleviating poverty and improving the lives of people on welfare.

Since then, Ontario has been through a terrible economic recession. The recession is over, but there are still many Ontarians who have not recovered. They have not recovered the jobs they lost, the homes they lost, the security they lost. People living on welfare have had their benefits cut; eligibility requirements for both employment insurance and welfare have been tightened up. For people in need, things are now even bleaker than they were in 1990.

Almost everyone who came forward to speak at the Neighbour to Neighbour hearings talked about the struggle to maintain their dignity and self-respect while living in poverty, especially when the prevailing attitude seems to be that they are to blame for being poor. Living on a very low income is bad enough. What makes it so much worse is the feeling that society blames you—even despises you—for being in need.

"I don't think people realize what living like this does to a person," Patricia told us at one community hearing. "It's not just a matter of going without. It's what it does to a person emotionally, physically and spiritually. All sense of hope is taken away. You become oppressed and can no longer function. You suffer physically because you are not eating, emotionally because social contact is lost, spiritually because all hope is gone."

In what was perhaps a symbolic moment, a candidate seeking re-election in the spring federal election came to a hearing and sat at the back of the room, listening quietly. He presently fell asleep, while listening to the stories (thus becoming a recumbent candidate). Afterward, during a break, he got up and spoke on television about his party's vision of how they would respond to the blight of poverty. He demonstrated nicely the practice of much governing that affects people who happen

When there is hunger while some have too much to eat, or when there is homelessness while some live in luxury, or when there is poverty in the midst of affluence, justice is not present.

to have low incomes—listening to their views and experiences rarely seems to have a place in decision-making that will deeply affect their lives.

There are a few things the reader should know about the personal accounts from low-income people documented in this publication.

Several hundred people attended these hearings, to speak and to listen. We have tried to include enough personal accounts to give a good sampling of what we heard. But we could have filled several more volumes with the stories, ideas and concerns of those who came forward.

The comments and stories have been edited and are usually excerpted from longer presentations. We have taken care to retain the intent and flavour of the stories. A few of the comments quoted are from people who work in community organizations, social service agencies or faith groups. They are identified as such. *To protect personal privacy, people's names have been changed and no place names are used. The stories are real. They come from real people, living in our communities.*

Between the chapters are stories that illustrate many of the main themes that emerged during the hearings… the loss of dignity… the fear and desperation when there is no money to cover basic necessities… the anger and guilt that children are being deprived of what all kids need to have a good start in life… the frustration of searching for work and not finding a job… the feeling of betrayal by one's own community and government… the exhaustion and alienation that come from eking out a living on so little.

We have organized the chapters around major issues that emerged from the hearings:

- Poverty and public policy
- Living on welfare
- Searching for work at a living wage
- The necessities of life
- The health factor
- Moms and kids
- How should we respond?

To help Ontarians better understand the scope of poverty, this book provides some statistics on poverty. But this is not primarily a sociological study of poverty or an analysis of social policy. Our major thrust is to help Ontarians better understand what it's like to fall on hard times and have to ask for help. Therefore, this book presents snapshots of life from the perspective of our neighbours who know all too well what poverty looks like and feels like.

Several speakers at the hearings told of others who were too afraid to come. They feared repercussions from the system that is supposed to be supporting them at a time of need. They feared the judgmental attitudes of their neighbours, who do not understand what they are going through or why. But the willingness of large numbers of people to come and tell their stories bears witness to the sense of participation they still feel—even in the current social atmosphere. Angry or despairing words, though perhaps hard to hear, deserve our attention. They seek to recall the hearer to the understanding that we all, at some level, depend on each other.

Will we listen?

Sue's Story

My grief mounts daily. I grieve for families who will now never be able to escape from dangerous situations. I grieve for the youth who cannot believe in their leaders—those who are supposed to provide justice. I grieve for a province that can hear the objections of so many of its citizens and still ignore them. More than anything I grieve for the children...

Poverty is not a shame, but being ashamed of it is.

I am a community development worker and president of a local [city] Housing Tenant Association. I am also the wife of a terminally ill man and mother to a child with chronic learning disabilities, and although I work two part-time jobs, I am forced to be a recipient of government assistance.

The provincial government has forced many of my neighbours and their families to the brink of disaster. Henry Clay, the pre-Civil War U.S. statesman, said: "Government is a trust, and the officers are trustees: and both trust and trustees are created for the benefit of the people." I will try not to bore you with what you already know, but I feel very strongly about the federal and provincial governments' attempts to blame the economic problems of Canada on its less fortunate population.

My husband suffers with systemic lupus erythematosus. He must take seven different medications daily. Each one of these is covered by the government's assisted drug plan, but each prescription costs two dollars. He has worked since he was fifteen years old. Since the diagnosis in 1995 his quality of life has deteriorated rapidly. He was put on a provincial pension and was denied C.P.P. on the grounds that Lupus is "not severe or prolonged". We are appealing this denial.

We are currently trapped by a system that does not accept its populations as they truly are. There are days when my husband cannot walk, socialize or participate in any activities. In short, this man gets closer to death every day and is being left without hope or dignity for his future.

My son struggles daily to succeed in a system that is now designed not to help him overcome his challenges, but to ignore his needs and to squelch his potential to greatness. He will receive no assistance or encouragement to adapt, improvise and overcome his difficulties. His struggles will not be recognized and no solutions will be sought to advance him or the thousands like him. Provincial norms do not apply to this population nor will they ever be considered in the government's attempts to balance budgets; they will never be counted among the "useful of society."

In my capacity as president of the tenants' association, I live and work in a 172-townhouse family complex of rent-geared-to-income housing. During the three years that I have served as president, I have become more and more aware of the obstacles hampering those with income disparities, adults who now eat only one meal a day so that they can make their groceries last longer for their children, families who can no longer go out together on family outings, even small picnics, who cannot afford to go to a movie let alone the theatre. Most of the children I work with have never and now will probably never see a stage play.

Their parents suffer daily humiliations from government agencies which keep them on hold for an average wait of 11 minutes, the humiliation of telling their children that they have no money to send them on the class trips, the pain of not being able to get their children's school pictures, the mortification of not being able to send their children to school with a healthy packed lunch. There are teachers who marginalize their children because they come from a low-income housing complex.

Our society has been led to believe that people who are on assistance are not deserving of respect or opportunity, support or dignity. Neither the provincial nor the federal government considers the poor as viable or important populations. They are never consulted when policies are set down, especially those decisions that affect their quality of life.

Those suffering most are the working poor. I at least have access to medication when I need it; the working poor must choose very carefully when to treat their illnesses and those of their children. They make difficult choices daily and in most cases they pay rents well over 40% of their monthly incomes.

Since the onset of the government's "Common Sense Revolution" the only sense has been a sense of hopelessness, despair, desperation, anguish, disenfranchisement and isolation. Community agencies have been so burdened with the cries for help that in many cases there is no place to send people. Families once self-sufficient and stable are approaching agencies for relief that they cannot find.

Food banks, which were unheard of in the 1970s, are in every city. Access to these services are restricted. Most food banks can only be accessed monthly or tri-monthly. The need for social agencies is on the rise and yet funding is being torn away. This government has decided that churches and non-profit agencies should deliver social services with no financial assistance from government. Workers at these agencies are crying out about the effects of the cuts but their cries are falling on deaf ears...

CHAPTER 2

Poverty and Public Policy

Everyone has the right to a standard of living adequate to the health and well-being of himself [herself] and his [her] family, including food, clothing, housing, and medical care and necessary social services, and the right to security in the event of unemployment, sickness, disability, widowhood, old age, or other loss of livelihood in circumstances beyond his [her] control.

Article 25, The Universal Declaration of Human Rights

The Universal Declaration of Human Rights was adopted and proclaimed by the UN General Assembly in 1948. It was a milestone in recognizing a global standard for the protection of the human community. The Declaration was followed over the years by a number of other international covenants, which Canada has signed.

In 1976, our federal government, after reaching agreement with the provinces, signed the International Covenant on Economic, Social and Cultural Rights, which affirmed:

- the inherent dignity of the human person;
- the right of everyone to an adequate standard of living, including adequate food, clothing, and housing;
- the right of everyone to work and gain a living by work of one's own choosing;
- the right to enjoy the highest attainable physical and mental health; and
- the right to education.

By signing this Covenant, governments in Canada and the other signatory nations agreed to take steps to the maximum of their resources to achieve the "full realization" of these rights. What has happened to our promises?

Many Canadians are enjoying a high standard of living and quality of life. But there is a substantial segment of the population that is suffering severe economic hardship and experiencing a deteriorating quality of life.

In a country that consistently ranks at or near the top of the United Nations' Human Development Index, which measures factors such as life expectancy and per capita income, it is hard to understand why we are not making progress in reducing poverty. Measured on how well we are doing in alleviating the incidence and severity of poverty, Canada ranks far below first. According to the UN, we are 10th out of the 17 wealthiest nations in the world.

As a nation, we are not living up to our international covenants to ensure that all citizens have the opportunity to participate fully in our society.

As neighbours, we are tolerating the fact that our fellow Canadians do not have a standard a living that is adequate for their health and well-being and that of their children. The latest figures from the National Council of Welfare, the federally-appointed citizens' advisory body that monitors poverty, show that 17.6% or almost 5.2 million Canadians, including 1,481,000 children, were living in poverty across this country in 1996.[1]

And the poor are getting poorer. The National Council of Welfare noted that Statistics Canada figures for 1996 show that the average family incomes of Canadians changed little between 1995 and 1996. But total incomes of the poorest 20 percent of Canadians "dropped dramatically because of a combination of lower earnings and cuts to cash transfers from governments."[2]

The focus of this book is poverty in Ontario. It is important to understand, however, that what is happening to the poor in Ontario is part of a national trend. Poverty is a national disgrace.

In 1996, the poverty rate in Ontario was 15.8% or 1,770,000 people. Around a million of those people, including children, relied on social assistance. The rest relied on income from the labour market. Consider these statistics:

- The poverty rate in 1996 was the highest it has been since the mid-1980s. It was actually higher in 1996 than it was during the last recession in the early 1990s.[3]

- The number of children living in poverty in this province has increased to about half a million, an increase of 99% in eight years.[4]

1 National Council of Welfare, *Poverty Profile 1996*, Ottawa, 1998. The poverty statistics are based on Statistics Canada Low-Income Cut-Offs.
2 National Council of Welfare, *Poverty Profile 1996*, based on Statistics Canada, Income Distribution by Size in Canada, 1996.
3 National Council of Welfare, *Poverty Profile 1996*.
4 Ontario Campaign 2000, *Child Poverty in Ontario, Report Card 1997*, Toronto.

- About one-third of poor children lived in families whose parents have the equivalent of a full-time job, but don't earn enough to stay out of poverty.[5]

The numbers are shocking enough in themselves. But the trend is more frightening still. *Poverty is worsening—not in a time of recession, but in a time of economic growth.* Figure 1 shows the incidence of poverty in Ontario from 1980 through 1996.

Figure 1

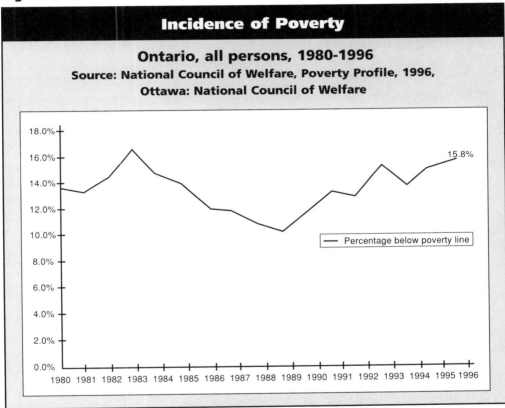

Poverty in Ontario is also deepening. The poverty line we are using is based on the Statistics Canada Low-Income Cut-Offs (LICO), which are the most commonly accepted measures of poverty. They are calculated using what the average Canadian family spends on the basics of food, shelter and clothing, with a fixed percentage for other necessities, such as transportation. The amounts are adjusted for community and family size. The value of this type of measurement of low income is that it is related to the reality of life in Canada—what people have to pay for food and rent, for example—not some measure of the cost of keeping people alive.

5 Ontario Campaign 2000, *Child Poverty in Ontario, Report Card 1997*, Toronto.

Figure 2 shows just how close to bare subsistence some people among us are living. Just over 12% of lone-parent families in 1996 lived on less than half of a poverty-line income.[6]

Figure 2

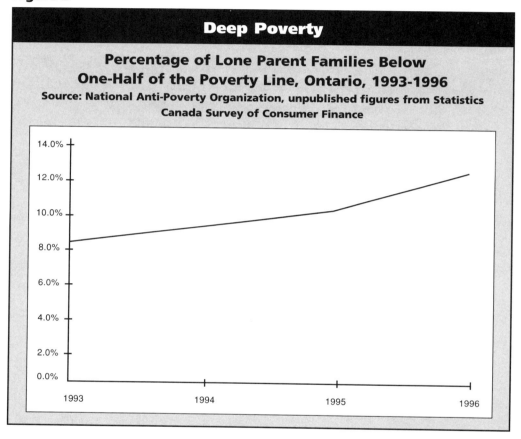

What is Behind These Statistics?

One major factor is unemployment. Although unemployment has been declining since the last recession at the start of the decade, it is still relatively high. During 1997, when the Neighbour to Neighbour hearings were held, unemployment in Ontario was 8.5%. It has stayed above 7% in 1998.

Another factor is the type of employment that is available. Among those who have jobs, the restructuring of the economy has increased part-time employment and contract or temporary work, making it harder for many people to earn a living wage

6 National Anti-Poverty Organization, from unpublished figures from Statistics Canada.

and increasing the numbers of Ontarians moving in and out of paid work. Many Ontarians are underemployed, doing work that does not use their qualifications and experience.

But we can't just blame the spread and deepening of poverty on globalization of the economy and throw up our hands. Because part of the answer is that we have chosen to make it so. Governments, acting on our behalf, have opened up large holes in the social safety net—a social safety net that has been woven together, with the wide support of Canadians, since the Great Depression.

For example, the Ontario government has:

- reduced welfare benefits and shelter allowances by 21.6% for all social assistance recipients, including those with children, except those who are categorized as disabled or who are over 65; welfare rates have been held at this reduced level for three years now, as the cost of living continues to rise;

- frozen the minimum wage, which means that the value of the minimum wage is being allowed to erode as the cost of living continues to rise.

> **The numbers are shocking enough in themselves. But the trend is more frightening still. Poverty is worsening—not in a time of recession, but in a time of economic growth.**

The federal government is also complicit. Its actions may have been more indirect, but it has contributed to the erosion of social programs in Ontario and across Canada, first by de-funding them and then by removing national standards.

Under the Canada Assistance Plan (CAP), the federal government provided 50% of the funding of welfare and social services to the provinces. In return, the provinces were required to provide assistance based on need and at adequate levels; refrain from making work for benefits (workfare) obligatory; make benefits available to Canadians regardless of province of residency; and provide a system of appeals for those wishing to challenge decisions about eligibility or the amount of benefits.

In 1990, as Canada entered a recession, the federal government limited its contributions under the CAP to increases of five per cent per year for Ontario, British Columbia, and Alberta. By 1993, instead of cost-sharing 50-50, it was paying only 28 per cent of welfare costs in Ontario. By the end of 1995, the cap on CAP had cost Ontario $8.4 billion.[7]

7 National Council of Welfare, *Another Look at Welfare Reform*, 1997.

Having eroded CAP, the federal government unilaterally eliminated it in 1996, and replaced it with the Canada Health and Social Transfer, which puts funding for social assistance, health, and post-secondary education all in the same pool. There are no conditions on how this money is to be used. The only national standard for welfare retained under the Canada Health and Social Transfer is the right not to be discriminated against because of residency. The door has opened for the gutting of social assistance systems across Canada.

The federal government has also reduced and restricted the Employment Insurance program in an economy that is

Governments, acting on our behalf, have opened up large holes in the social safety net—a social safety net that has been woven together, with the wide support of Canadians, since the Great Depression.

progressively more oriented to short-term contract labour. Not only have the level and duration of employment benefits been reduced considerably, but many workers and their families who previously would have been covered by EI during times of unemployment have been forced to turn to social assistance. There has been an astounding decrease in the proportion of unemployed Canadians covered by the program—from 88 per cent in 1990 to 43 per cent in mid-1997.[8]

In fact, readers will learn from the stories in this book that many of the people who are now numbered among the poorest of the poor in our province were once middle-income working people who never dreamed they would end up on welfare. Brenda describes her situation:

How does one join the ranks of poverty? Some may be born into it and it becomes very difficult to escape its bondage. For women, we can suddenly find ourselves living a life that we had never dreamed possible—suddenly we are poor. For many of us, it came as a result of domestic violence when as a last resort we had to leave our homes and start over in new cities far away from our homes, families and friends.

I speak of this from personal experience. Growing up in a middle-class working family, there was never any other way of doing things but to earn our way in life. I was working full-time at sixteen years old, married in my twenties, and continued to work until my children were born, after which I baby-sat from home to earn money. And then one day it all ended. Domestic violence made

8 National Council of Welfare, *Another Look at Welfare Reform*, 1997.

The federal government has also reduced and restricted the Employment Insurance program in an economy that is progressively more oriented to short-term contract labour.

it too dangerous for us to remain in Montreal. With $30 in my pocket, my two children and I escaped to Toronto.

Our first home here for seven weeks was a shelter, and then came the realization that there were no jobs that I was qualified for, and that I would have to rely on welfare. I ended up having a breakdown and was in hospital for three weeks. After my release, came the formidable task of finding a place to live. Rents were (are) astronomical, waiting lists for public housing years long, and then I had to come up with first and last months' rent. We are now settled in a basement apartment where the rent is more than in the four-bedroom townhouse that we were renting in Montreal.

Then comes food. There is never enough left for food especially with three growing children. Food banks are not easily accessible in my neighbourhood and my one experience was so embarrassing that I would not repeat it again, so often my children eat and I do not. Now the government wants to implement workfare. Yes, it is good to work. Two years ago, I was fortunate enough to get a job in retail. But because of my low income it means often walking one hour to work and one hour back because there is not enough for transportation and child care…Women like me also have to face our children who are often ostracized at school for being poor.

I would like to tell the government that I am intelligent, bilingual, and would be an asset to any company that would take a chance and hire me. I would be especially good with people who have suffered as I did. Also my children are hard-working. I know that in spite of all that the government is doing to make it difficult for us, my children will succeed.

Brenda

Social Reinvestment

Whenever the issue of poverty arises, there are always some who say we cannot afford to do anything about it. If there is to be a fiscal dividend, they say, it must be used for tax cuts or debt reduction. But our governments have balanced their budgets at least in part by cutting transfers to the most vulnerable in our society.

Now that public sector deficits have been reduced or all but eliminated, it is time to reinvest in the social infrastructure of our society.

In Ontario, families who are among the poorest of the poor are having the amount of their child benefit deducted from their welfare cheques.

We recognize that the federal government has made some effort to address the poverty of children of the working poor through the new National Child Benefit System. But the agreement reached between the federal and provincial/territorial governments allowed provinces to claw back the benefits from parents on welfare. In Ontario, families who are among the poorest of the poor are having the amount of their child benefit deducted from their welfare cheques. The provinces agreed to reinvest the money that they claw back from welfare families in programs and services for low-income families with children. For example, Ontario has announced new programs to help parents with child care expenses. But the families who are affected by the claw-back are not necessarily going to be the same families who are helped by the new programs.

Furthermore, these efforts are basically nibbling around the edges of the problem— particularly when governments see fit to juggle expenditures within the "poverty envelope" i.e. use money from one group of poor families to provide programs for another. ISARC believes we should confront the poverty problem head-on.

Ruth's Story

I still feel shame at not having a job. I keep looking for work in [this] area, the Toronto area, and out west. I've developed six resumes which I use. I feel the loss of life purpose. I have a constant inner struggle to do a full-time job search, get exercise to keep depression at bay. Sometimes I feel lower than a worm in a wheel rut.

My name is [Ruth], and I'm 41 years old. I finished high school and went on to complete four years of university and earned my Bachelor of Social Work degree. The first course I ever took in social work was entitled Common Human Needs.

I have worked full time for approximately 15 years for a variety of social service organizations, and I have lived in northern and central Ontario, Toronto, Calgary, northern Alberta, and Halifax. My moves were to pursue employment, and the challenges that employment gave me. I was financially independent, I was employed in my chosen profession, social work. My Monday-to-Friday life was full.

I paid all my bills, bought groceries, enjoyed the odd movie or play, swam daily, did my professional reading, had relationships with clients, other professionals, and friends, did personal growth work, and saved for my retirement. All this changed on a September day in 1995. I had been unemployed for a year, my finances were depleted and I was desperate.

My only alternative was to apply for social assistance, otherwise known as welfare. I had previously applied to work for them, never dreaming that I'd be on this side of the desk. A worker came into my home, which I own, prodded into every aspect of my financial life, and looked at me very skeptically when I responded that I was single and lived alone. My life was assessed in dollars and cents, and I was told that I would qualify as a single unemployed employable person. I was given a list of expectations of what I must and must not do.

I would receive $520 a month, or $6,240 a year. I believe the poverty line is now around $13,000 a year. Thus I'd be living $6,760 under the poverty line, an utterly depressing situation. At the same time in 1995, our Premier decided to scrap photo radar. This boggled my mind. I saw photo radar as a reasonable, socially responsible way to collect money. People who broke the law by speeding on our highways would be under surveillance, they'd be issued a fine, and we'd have additional monies in the Province's coffers. But this didn't happen. Instead, the people who were breaking the law went scot free, and the people who were out of work, and with limited financial choices were punished by having their social assistance cheque reduced. Justice?

About this time, the Minister of Transportation reduced winter road maintenance, and told the public if we had problems we could simply place a call on our cellular phones. Never have I felt so angry at the lack of awareness of the realities of middle and low-income Ontario residents. When such attitudes are presented from the height of our parliamentary system, they flow through society, and further negate the truth that poverty exists, that we are not all living equally. The basic belief in community and helping one another is undermined.

As I saw it, the line was firmly drawn. It was them—Social Services, representing the provincial government—against me, someone who happened to be unemployed and out of choices. After my initial interview I felt rage, anger, depression, bitterness, and a sense of hopelessness. I was ashamed that I had to apply for welfare, ashamed that I didn't have a job, and ashamed of being poor. Because welfare did not give me enough to live on, I felt that I did not deserve any better. The lack of healthy food led to depression and the downward spiral continued.

The main expectation for a single unemployed employable receiving benefits is to conduct a job search during normal working hours from Monday to Friday. The social assistance system must realize people need help with self-esteem if they have been unemployed for even a short time. A lot of my identity is tied up with my employment. I can define my role in society when I work, being able in part to say who I am by what I do. When employment ceases, one can end up in emotional, social and physical difficulty just dealing with that, let alone the loss of income.

While I have been on social assistance, I've experienced stress in every aspect of my life. Being poor is a full-time job in itself. I always lack money to pay the mortgage, utilities, home and car insurance and food. People who were friends now don't call. Many don't know how long their jobs will be there, and they don't want to be reminded what could happen. There is no money for diversions, movie rentals, or a cup of coffee with friends unless they buy. Shopping, cooking and eating become major time consumers. Convenience foods cost too much. Applying for a job in person is really difficult. I have to make sure my sense of self-esteem is way up. Explain what I have been doing while I was unemployed? It would be nice to say I volunteer, but that is difficult when doing a full-time job search, unless it's at night, and by then my energy is depleted.

I feel dependent. I'm treated like I'm guilty until proven innocent, and the general public still thinks that we are lazy welfare bums. I worked part-time over the Christmas season. I've tried a number of ways to make a living. I took an entrepreneur's course, ran a home-based lunch business, did house cleaning, worked on the census, and most recently at a retail store. I've taken work when I could get it, but I still don't seem to get ahead at all. In fact, every time I work and pay off some debts, I seem to get penalized by the welfare system, either having my benefits cut off altogether, or getting further reduced benefits when the normal monthly benefits are not enough to live on anyway.

I still feel shame at not having a job. I keep looking for work in [this] area, the Toronto area, and out west. I've developed six resumes which I use. I feel the loss of life purpose. I have a constant inner struggle to do a full-time job search, get exercise to keep depression at bay. Sometimes I feel lower than a worm in a wheel rut. It gets bad on the days when I decide it doesn't matter, there's no point even trying. If I'm lucky on those days, I remember to do a reality check.

I have some thoughts on how to improve the system.

- Change the emphasis from a punitive attitude to one of support towards those who must utilize the system. To do this, workers must look at clients from a holistic viewpoint. No good is served by looking solely at finances. The system must become more than an income maintenance tool.

- Provide enough income so that each day is not a struggle, and people can meet their common human needs. Cover preventive health costs, such as dental work.

- Become more realistic about the labour market. We do not have a fertile job market. Make it worthwhile for a recipient to accept work, whether it be casual, seasonal, part-time or full-time.

- Encourage those who would like to start their own businesses. Now a single unemployed person may work toward establishing a business, but they must continue with a job search. It's an impossible task.

- Scrap the idea of workfare. Public attitudes to welfare are negative enough without putting us in a situation where we are taking our fellow citizens' jobs.

- Look at new alternatives, like a 30-34 hour work week. My understanding is that if people worked the above hours, and employers hired new workers complete with benefits, we could be well on our way to solving our unemployment problem. Companies do not want to hire new workers because of the cost of benefits, training, etc. We could develop tax incentives to encourage hiring.

I'm an educated healthy woman who should once again be given the opportunity to become financially independent and gain my self-respect back. After all, it is a common human need.

CHAPTER 3

Living on Welfare

Most of us do not have sufficient incomes to pay our rent and to eat properly, even when we try to manage our resources by bargaining for dented tins of tuna. So how are we supposed to afford bus fare to get to whatever programs we might be sent to for our own good?

Peter

About one million of the 1.7 million poor people in Ontario rely on social assistance or welfare.

Whenever the issue of welfare comes up, there are always some who say that recipients need a push to get them off the system. The push, in this context, usually means less money to live on so welfare won't be too comfortable, and some form of compulsory work-for-welfare or workfare.

Those who experienced a 21.6% reduction in benefits in 1995 told the Neighbour to Neighbour hearings in communities across Ontario what this financial incentive did for them. They became poorer and more desperate. Many of them were working part-time, and trying to find a permanent full-time job again. But job searches and interviews were made more difficult by the sheer grind of daily poverty and the depression that comes from feelings of humiliation and hopelessness. Rather than helping them get off welfare, the "push" of greater poverty has made it more difficult to break free.

Many members of the public apparently supported a general crackdown on welfare. It was one of the campaign promises of the current provincial government—to reduce welfare costs and institute workfare—and they were elected. People on welfare are living in conditions many of us have never experienced. They are neighbours many of us have never met. We ask our fellow Ontarians to listen to accounts of the hardship that so many individuals and families with children have experienced. And to think about what happens to people who are turned down for welfare—what options do they have left except living on the street?

What Is a Welfare Income?

Welfare poverty has deepened since what welfare provides was reduced by 21.6% in October of 1995 for all recipients but the disabled and people over 65. The first full year after the cuts was 1996. Figure 3 shows the annual benefits of welfare recipients, and what has happened to those benefits since 1986, expressed in 1996

Figure 3

Annual Welfare Benefits in Constant (1996) Dollars				
Ontario 1986-1996 Source: National Council of Welfare, Welfare Incomes 1996.				
	Single Employable	Disabled Person	Single Parent/One Child	Couple/Two Children
1986	$6,955		$12,456	$15,505
1989	$7,474	$10,791	$13,413	$16,927
1990	$8,116	$11,520	$15,042	$19,737
1991	$8,371	$11,760	$15,394	$20,081
1992	$8,669	$11,969	$15,691	$20,540
1993	$8,638	$11,898	$15,663	$20,483
1994	$8,634	$11,890	$15,657	$20,286
1995	$8,024	$11,650	$14,535	$18,716
1996	$6,584	$11,466	$11,940	$15,428

dollars. For example, benefits for a single parent with one child dropped from $15,657 in 1994 to $11,940 in 1996. Under the current rates, a single non-disabled employable person receives just $6,584 year. A single disabled person receives $11,466.

Figure 4 shows welfare incomes (which include tax credits like the Child Tax Credit) as a percentage of the poverty line from 1986 to 1996. For example, the income of a single parent with one child was 63% of a poverty-line income in 1996. A single person was at 42% of a poverty-line income.

Figure 4

Welfare Incomes as a Percentage of the Poverty Line				
Ontario 1986-1996 Source: National Council of Welfare, Welfare Incomes 1996.				
	Single Employable	Disabled Person	Single Parent/One Child	Couple/Two Children
1986	43%		64%	58%
1989	47%	68%	68%	61%
1990	52%	72%	76%	70%
1991	54%	75%	79%	72%
1992	55%	76%	80%	73%
1993	55%	76%	80%	73%
1994	55%	76%	80%	72%
1995	51%	74%	75%	67%
1996	42%	73%	63%	57%

ISARC realizes that there are people who like to debate what constitutes poverty in a rich country like Canada. We think it is more appropriate for Ontarians to consider how they would personally get by if they had to live on these incomes.

Welfare rates include what is paid for shelter and for the rest of the living expenses of the individual or family. The box (Figure 5) on page 36, shows the welfare benefits and shelter, on a monthly basis pre- and post- reductions from October, 1995.

Surviving on Welfare

The two stories that follow illustrate what some people do to survive from month to month on a welfare income.

What is it like to be on Social Assistance? I receive $957 a month, plus $102 Baby Bonus on the 20th of each month. By the second of the month, $800 is gone on rent and bills, leaving $259 for:

- food (my daughter and I)
- diapers
- personal items—shampoo, dish soap, laundry powder, garbage bags, etc.
- any emergencies—e.g. pedialyte to prevent dehydration, bandaids, etc.
- transportation—buses, taxis, etc.

I don't smoke, drink or take drugs. I've never been to a bingo hall or the casino. I have no social life. I don't go to parties and I rarely go to a coffee shop. My

Figure 5

Ontario Social Assitance Monthly Benefits

Rates Before October 1995

	Basic Allowance	Maximum Shelter Allowance	Maximum Total
Single	$249	$414	$663
Single Parent + 1 child*	$569	$652	$1,221
Couple +2 children**	$781	$768	$1,549
Single Disabled	$516	$414	$930
Disabled spouse +2 children**	$1,048	$768	$1,816

Rates Effective October 1995

	Basic Allowance	Maximum Shelter Allowance	Maximum Total
Single	$195	$325	$520
Single Parent + 1 child*	$446	$511	$957
Couple +2 children**	$612	$602	$1,214
Single Disabled	$516	$414	$930
Disabled spouse +2 children**	$1,048	$768	$1,816

* child under 12, ** one child over twelve

only concern is my daughter and giving her the best life that I can—which doesn't include sitting on social assistance for the rest of my life. I struggle to pay my bills. Some months it is impossible to pay all of them so I fall behind and then have to deal with the stress of trying to catch up. Why do I fall behind?

- Trying to find money to buy clothes/shoes for a child who constantly grows out of them;
- Trying to keep nutritious meals on the table every day;
- Getting around—I don't own a car, can't afford to buy a wagon to pull her in, and my stroller is on its last legs.

I also have no family support. To get groceries I either make several trips back and forth to the store until I get all that I need, or I spread it over several days if the weather is good, or I walk one way, and take a taxi back. Keep in mind, with no extra money available for transport, any extra expenses have to be taken from money set aside to pay bills.

I never have the opportunity to take advantage of sales, nor do I have enough money to shop for specials anyway. Added expenses are often impossible to deal with. For example, I cannot afford to replace my frying pan which burnt out two months ago. I even run out of money trying to keep up with the laundry.

I can't afford to take my daughter on special trips. I know I'll struggle with day care costs when it

I deal with the prejudice and hostility that are directed towards people on social assistance because people believe the myth that we don't want to work. As if I really want poverty as a career choice for my beautiful daughter and me.

comes time to register her, if she'll even be able to go. I know I'll never be able to let her join sports or bowling or dance. This doesn't bother me as much as it does knowing that the everyday necessities are becoming more of a struggle to provide. The stress is unbelievable at times. I am with my daughter constantly, 24 hours a day, 7 days a week. No breaks, no time for myself. I cannot afford a babysitter.

No sense of security—I live month to month—wondering if I'm going to lose my home because I can't afford the rent. I can't accumulate any kind of savings to cover the unexpected or for my daughter's future, e.g. education, dental expenses. Sometimes I run out before the end of the month and I have to go to the food banks or St. Vincent de Paul for a food voucher—neither one of which makes you feel better about yourself. Both of these groups make you feel like a loser. It's humiliating. Every day I wake up depressed and stressed out, hoping nothing will go wrong, because I have no money to deal with it anyway.

I deal with the prejudice and hostility that are directed towards people on social assistance because people believe the myth that we don't want to work. As if I really want poverty as a career choice for my beautiful daughter and me.

I do not fear hardship, but I am afraid of what I see. I belonged to Amnesty International for five years, I sent over 400 letters protesting human rights abuses. My areas of concern were Central and South America. There, the poor were abandoned by their governments—targets of human rights abuses and death squads because they were the "undesirable" ones of society. We too have been abandoned as undesirable by all levels of government. I think it is very sad.

Rosemary

I am among the lucky ones in this community. I have a place to live, food to eat, and clothes to wear, which though worn are still serviceable. I also have one more very important asset. I share costs with a friend, without whose help mine would be a very different story.

Each month, I must take $45 out of my food money to cover the rest of my share of the rent. That's $90 between us that could go towards better food, clothing, or an emergency. We are all told to eat healthier. How? The better the quality or freshness of the food, the higher the cost, so you buy what you can afford, not what is necessarily the best choice. Also, heaven help us if we get sick and must buy over-the-counter medications, or those medications which health plans don't cover. As for the dentist, you can go only in the most dire of emergencies, because you can't afford the difference between what it costs and what welfare pays. It's the same with glasses.

Think about this. If you have $242 a month for food, that budget has to cover not only food but the $45 extra for the rent, $29 for phone, $25 for medication that you must have, $6 for prescription medications, $7 for cleaning supplies. That totals $112.

That leaves $130 a month or $4.33 a day for food. Please note, that clothing, and personal hygiene items are not listed. As I said, I'm lucky, I'm not alone, I can fall back on my friends and faith. I pity those who can't.

Linda

Many others explained their personal finances and, almost invariably, they spoke of having to cut out or cut down on basics: to eat less food and less nourishing food, pay rents up to 80% of their income, or move to inadequate housing. Some spoke of moving back to a town with fewer job prospects but with stronger family and friendships. They also spoke of depression, anxiety, frustration, and rage. Above all, they spoke with gritty perseverance, an unwillingness to let hardship get the best of them. As Brent, a young man in Kitchener who has lived on the street, said: "I'm a survivor."

Here is another account of strategies for dealing with the loss of income:

Drink more water to help eliminate hunger, cut out daughter's bus pass. She walks. Do laundry less often, get bread at Salvation Army instead of buying. Sometimes there is no bread though. Cannot ask for food. Shame is too great. Take self-esteem classes and counselling. Buy jigsaw puzzles at low prices to help with stress. Don't listen to radio call-in shows that discuss what's happening affecting our situation. Try to keep close to God and turn anger into compassion and understanding. Try to get other people who can see things better to help me. Read lots of helpful books. Count on outside services more, such as church, art centre, counselling. I wear the same clothes all the time because my daughter is a teenager and I want her to feel good about herself. I can go without because the peer pressure is not like it is when you're a teenager. I cannot give to others.

Gwen

Changes to Welfare

The social assistance system in Ontario has recently undergone major changes. The old assistance programs—Family Benefits (FBA) and General Welfare (GWA)—have been replaced by two new programs: Ontario Works and the Ontario Disability Support Program.

When the Neighbour to Neighbour hearings were held, the legislation that set the framework and enabled implementation of the new programs was going through the legislative process. The Social Assistance Reform Act was passed in November 1997, and was proclaimed (and therefore came into force) in stages during 1998.

Because all of this is new, most recipients whose stories are included in this book still refer to being on Family Benefits (sometimes called Mother's Allowance) or General Welfare.

Most sole-support mothers and people with disabilities received Family Benefits, and people classified as employable were on General Welfare. These distinctions are now removed. Recipients are going to be in the Ontario Works program, and subject to its requirements for workfare—taking education and training, performing a community service or other work placement, or getting a job—or they are going to be in the Disability Support Program. At the time of printing, the process of moving people into the new programs was underway. However, because of a new comprehensive verification process, some people were being screened out of the welfare system before they could transfer to the new programs.

A profound shift in philosophy has taken place. The old programs were founded in entitlement to assistance based on need and a recognition of the community's responsibility to those in need. The new Ontario Works program puts the onus on the individual to achieve self-reliance through employment.

Participation in workfare is mandatory unless a person qualifies for a temporary deferral. For example, a single parent with a child for whom publicly-funded education is not available may get a deferral. If there is a junior kindergarten, however, parents of children as young as three may be required to participate.

The provincial government used to administer the Family Benefits program, while municipalities administered General Welfare. Administration of Ontario Works which includes welfare and FB sole support parents is the responsibility of municipalities, while the Ontario Disability Support Program which replaces FB disability benefits continues to be administered by the province. As well, the Province has given itself major new powers to change the rules of both these new programs through regulations.

Because new regulations have been coming out all year, it was not possible at the time of printing to give a very clear explanation of how it is all going to work. This confusion has not only made life more frightening for poor people, it has also caused difficulties for municipalities trying to administer the new programs, and for social and other community agencies trying to assist low-income people. Here are just a few of the changes:

- There are stricter conditions for emergency assistance, which has traditionally involved providing small amounts of money to get people over a crisis.

- Liens will be put on people's houses if they stay on welfare for more than 12 months. There are new rules for adults who live in their parents' home.

- The monetary value of goods and services received is counted as income. This means that if family or friends provide food or meals over a period of time, the value must be reported and it will be deducted from the person's welfare cheque. Gifts, payments of small value, and food from food banks are still exempt.

- The Support to Employment Program (STEP), which allows people who work to retain a portion of their earnings while on welfare, is being curtailed. After working for a year, a person will be able to keep 20% of what they earn after the basic exemption (instead of the previous 25%), and the amount will continue to drop (15% after two years, 10% after three) until it reaches zero after five years.

- The $37 a month extra that pregnant women used to receive for six months has been officially eliminated. However, a pregnant woman can ask for a special diet allowance, which she may or may not get through the municipality.

- The "buffer zone" which allowed some working poor people to get a drug card to cover necessary prescriptions even if they earned slightly more than the welfare limit ($50 more for singles, $100 more for families) has been eliminated.

- New powers have been given to Eligibility Review Officers to demand information and conduct searches for evidence of fraud.

What is the general message that the system is sending? It is a get-tough approach. People are going to have a harder time getting assistance, and once on assistance, welfare will operate more like a loan program than a income support program. Recipients will be monitored more closely on the assumption that many of them are going to cheat.

A Loss of Dignity

There is one message that came through more clearly than any other in the Neighbour to Neighbour hearings. It was that people who rely on income support from government feel they are devalued as human beings.

The feeling comes from the apparent acceptance by the general public that living on welfare has been too easy, and therefore a reduction of almost 22% in income was an appropriate policy decision. The feeling comes from the preoccupation with welfare fraud in the media and in government—as though everyone in need is out to cheat the system. It comes from the much-used rhetoric these days that many people on welfare shouldn't be there—they don't need the help or they don't deserve it, and they won't get off the system unless they are forced out.

The International Covenant on Economic, Social, and Cultural Rights recognizes "the inherent dignity of the human person". Time and again during the hearings, people spoke of how their worst pain came from their sense of being blamed for many social problems. They described the difficult task they face sometimes simply maintaining a sense of dignity in the face not only of material hardship, but also messages coming from many different directions that their poverty is their own fault.

Loss of dignity cannot be quantified the way social assistance rates or rents can be, but it is as real. Below, Joanne talks about being made to feel like a second-class citizen.

I went on general welfare in February 1995. I'd been out of work for about half a year. My last job had been short in duration and low paying. I didn't qualify for unemployment insurance after it ended. The prospect of going on welfare was frightening to me and I made my savings last as long as I absolutely could before applying.

Once I had been on welfare for a couple of months, my initial fears subsided. I felt that, although it was not pleasant, at least it was bearable. I continued my job search. My relief didn't last very long. June 1995 brought to power the only government ever whose election promises had seemed to me to be more worthy of being called election threats. First came the pain of feeling that society was blaming me for something that was not my fault. I'd tried and tried to find work, but I just couldn't get anyone to hire me. And now it seemed somehow official that I was a second-class citizen. It wasn't just some ignorant minority that felt that I was no good. It was now the majority in Ontario. It hurt so much that I ceased my involvement with two organizations because most of the people there were employed and well off. I'd heard unflattering comments about welfare recipients from individuals in each group.

And then the endless fear and worry and anger began. The anticipation of workfare. Not knowing exactly what was going to happen. I liked my volunteer job very much and I wanted to stay with it. I was not a lazy bum. I wanted a job

The old programs were founded in entitlement to assistance based on need and a recognition of the community's responsibility to those in need. The new Ontario Works program puts the onus on the individual to achieve self-reliance through employment.

very badly. I just didn't want anyone telling me how to spend my time while unemployed. I felt it should be my right to choose my own activities. The economy was improving so it seemed there was hope of getting a job. I was getting more interviews, but the months passed without a job offer. The stress was really taking a toll on my health. I was in bad shape by the spring of 1996.

My doctor mentioned that perhaps I should be on some antidepressant drug. Then she said that the drug she had in mind wasn't covered by welfare, so it wasn't an option. I said I didn't want to take a drug anyway. I just wanted to be left alone to run my own life.

The current welfare system seems based on distrust more than anything else. It seems to be assumed that if you are on welfare, you automatically want to cheat the system every way you can. Everything must be proven to the authorities about your income and other details of your situation. It feels like being a criminal. You have no financial privacy at all. People do illegal things in other areas of life and society takes precautions against it, usually in ways that do not demean people. Somehow, they should find a way to do the same in the area of welfare.

In the two years of my life on welfare since 1995, my health has been wrecked both physically and mentally. My job search has been sabotaged by the amount of stress I've been subjected to. I'm stressed out, disorganized and have great difficulty motivating myself to regularly check all the places that job openings might be advertised. I haven't been able to get many resumes sent out lately. It's hard to try to do well in job interviews under these conditions. My performance at my volunteer job and other activities has been adversely affected also. I'm not as well organized and I don't get as much work done in a given length of time as I could. This means that I have less to give to other people and I learn and gain experience for myself at a slower rate.

Joanne

It's not just the welfare system that is making people on social assistance feel distrusted and despised, as the following anecdote makes clear:

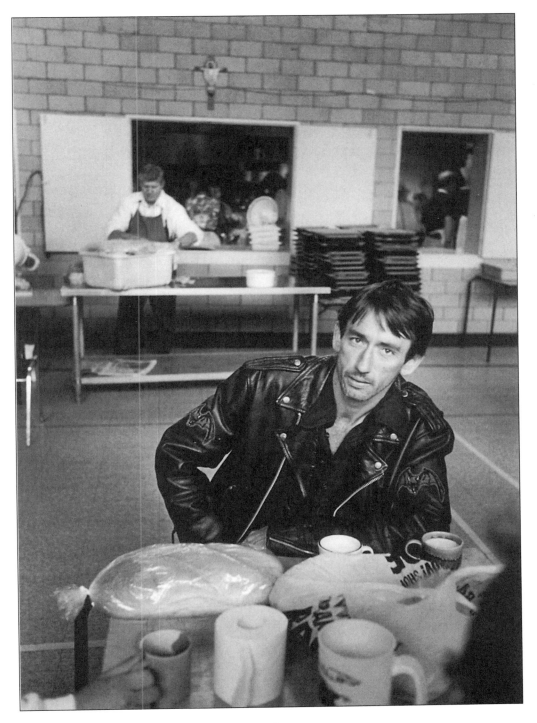

Time and again during the hearings, people spoke of how their worst pain came from their sense of being blamed for many social problems.

I would like speak a little bit about self-esteem. I had a cheque cashing card for the local grocery store that I had used many times. In the first few weeks I was on social assistance, a friend of mine asked if I would go to the grocery store and cash my cheque so I could loan her some money. They had made a mistake on her cheque, and she wasn't going to get it until late, and she was already out of diapers and baby formula and food for her other two children. I thought, well sure, she's really nice, I know she'll pay it back, and in a few days she'll have her cheque anyway. I was kind of embarrassed because I'd never done this before. The lady at the store picked it up, she looked at my cheque, she took my card and she cut it in half, right in front of everybody. And this woman at the back of the line, she was being really haughty, and snorting and whispering to the people at the back of the line. I felt this high. I was so humiliated.

If these people who criticized would just think that they are only one step away from problems themselves. If they lose their jobs or their health breaks down, or like me they leave an abusive relationship, their circumstances can change in a matter of minutes. Unemployment is only one step away from social assistance.

A lot of us feel like we're going through the Second Great Depression. And we're trying to survive. But the difference between this depression and the other is that there are lots of people out there that aren't hurting along with us. They're kind of leaving us behind and not caring. The banks and the corporations are getting more and more wealthy, while one in five children in Canada is in poverty. It just doesn't make sense.

Doris

Fraud in the welfare system is no more prevalent than it is in the income tax system, maybe less so. The generally accepted estimate from studies of income maintenance programs in Canada and other countries of the amount of improper payments—which include administrative errors by the system and honest mistakes by recipients, as well as fraud—is 2 to 5% of total payments. Why are we so preoccupied with snitch lines and crackdowns on welfare?

The next personal account is from Maxine, who tackles the myth that people make social assistance a "career choice":

I am fortunate to be here today and speak in past tense as a welfare recipient. I have been off the system for several months because of two factors: I was able to move into my partner's home with my daughter and I am employed for 34 hours a week with a temporary contract. What comes after that is cause for concern. No matter how much we may enjoy the kind of work we do as contract workers, it is certainly not known for

The current welfare system seems based on distrust more than anything else. It seems to be assumed that if you are on welfare, you automatically want to cheat the system every way you can.

future security or benefits. Chances of my going back on the system in the near future are unlikely because I am not on my own, but this too says a great deal.

Let's talk about actual dollars a family has to spend. During the months of September to November last year I found myself without any employment, leaving me and my child (who is a teenager) fully dependent on the system. The shelter allowance was $511 and my rent was $690. That left $287 from my basic allowance for food, telephone, school expenses, entertainment, clothing. The recommended amount for health to feed a single parent and child today is $75 a week. Already I was in the hole $13!

Forget about those other expenses. Looking at the numbers of actual dollars, there is no real safety net. Why do we as Canadians talk of a safety net, implying something secure is beneath us, a social system that all can depend on, when in reality that net has huge holes and does not hold us with a sense of entitlement at all? We no longer have a national standard.

Poor-bashing and snitch lines are a reality. Poor bashing comes from all sectors of society, including elected governments, as we have all witnessed in Ontario.

My intention is to give a face and a voice to the term welfare mom in order that we can begin dismantling the harmful, hateful myths that cover us. We are not a faceless mass. There is no typical welfare mom, no typical welfare recipient. Everyone has a story of how and why we ended up on the system. I am inviting everyone to recognize the complexities and the context of how we came to be here. We did not choose social assistance as a career choice.

I want to share with you my neighbour's comment about our laundry hanging on the clothes line. Dropping over to chat, I could see her surveying the line. We do not own pink or bright-coloured clothing but dark heavy pants, plaid shirts, tee shirts, the like. She asked if there was a man living with us.

When had he moved in? Imagine! She could have easily reported me [to welfare officials] over the colour and type of clothes my daughter and I wear!

I am sensing as the community shoulders more of the responsibility that we are dividing the deserving and the not-so-deserving. Single people on welfare are treated as if they do not have the same needs for nutrition, housing, or support systems. Those of us who find ourselves on assistance, underemployed or unemployed do contribute to our communities. We are the caretakers of your children, we are involved in school, sport, social committees, we are volunteers, we are lovers, we are your neighbours, friends and co-workers. Our story could easily be yours!

Poor-bashing and snitch lines are a reality. Poor bashing comes from all sectors of society, including elected governments, as we have all witnessed in Ontario.

Maxine

More than Dollars and Cents

A community support worker from Sudbury spoke from her perspective:

Life has become for many a vicious cycle of fear, hunger and exhaustion. So many families were terrified when the cuts came through. Mothers were heard screaming in the streets, "How am I going to make it? What am I going to do?" These screams have not gone away. People just don't hear them any more.

Folks who may not know what living poor is like may think that there are places for these poor families to go to for help; after all, there are food banks, clothing banks and shelters. But this is not entirely true. There are these organizations, but there is not enough. Not enough food, not enough warm clothes, and not enough beds. There's never enough money for these places to give whatever services they offer to all the many families that need them. I work with families who cannot go back to these organizations because they've had to go before. Don't get me wrong. These places will help many more times than just once, but they cannot help as often as some families require it.

Volunteer

As the volunteer who is quoted above concluded, just hearing about the dollars and cents that people struggle to live on isn't enough. Finances are only part of the story. Fear, shame, anger, depression and exhaustion are part of the "lived experience" for many people on welfare.

Claudette's Story

I'm a First Nations person. I spend a lot of time with the First Nations people here. My dream here is to start a Friendship Centre—a cultural centre for our urban native people. And I know myself right now of at least five native people who are living in this city and have no income. I've been here for 20 years and it's really hard, because you feel like aliens, walking down the street. The Centre would give them some place where they could go and talk to other people, have a hot bowl of soup, get job skills, life skills, whatever they would need.

I consider [this town] my home. I come from the First Nations [nearby]. I know how to live in poverty. We didn't have a lot but we were the richest poorest people. We had a home, which was more than a lot of other people.

For me, having to survive on welfare has been really difficult. I amaze myself how I do it. At one time, I was living in an abusive relationship, and I had three children. For my own safety, I had to leave. I didn't have my kids with me. I was told I would have them with me, but living on welfare, they would give me only enough for a single person, and in order for me to remain in contact with my kids, I had to have a two-bedroom apartment so that they could visit, so a lot of my money was going to pay for a two-bedroom apartment, which left me no food. When I did get the kids, I had no food.

Kids that come out of these homes have a lot of behaviour problems. I have one boy with me now. My partner is living with us, and we're required to do a job search, eh? We were both doing a job search, but because my son had so many behaviour problems, I had to school him at home. I couldn't look for work. Welfare didn't like [my partner's] job search, so they cut him off. We need a house because of my son's problems. We could not have gotten him under control any other way.

I don't consider that it [welfare] is charity. I really don't. My son's been a full-time job. And there is no way right now, with the amount of energy I've had to put into getting this kid squared away, that I could hold a job, because this boy needs me right now. That has to be my priority or else this kid is going to be out of hand in a few years.

I'm a First Nations person. I spend a lot of time with the First Nations people here. My dream here is to start a Friendship Centre—a cultural centre for our urban native people. And I myself right now know of at least five native people who are living in this city and have no income. I've been here for 20 years and it's really hard, because you feel like aliens, walking down the street. The Centre would give them some place where they could go and talk to other people, have a hot bowl of soup, get job skills, life skills, whatever they would need.

I'm getting $997 a month, and my rent is $550. My gas bills are $200, my hydro is at least $120. The rest buys food. I have a 13-year-old boy who wants a new skateboard, and I can't give it to him. I know it's hard on him, because he's made comments about being on welfare. I think he feels a lot of shame. It's hard to explain to him that there's just not enough. Even just last week we were in a real crunch.

When I was growing up we all helped each other. I'm feeling that's the only way I'm going to survive. We bring these other guys that have no income into the house, and we all try to eat together, because that's all that we can do. I grew up knowing how to cook hamburger in 200 different ways. Gee whiz, sometimes a pound of hamburger is feeding six or seven people. I grew up on fish and wild game. A pound of hamburger just doesn't go.

I feel like I'm just complaining. Sometimes it gets so hard that I think that I may have to move back to the reserve. I left because there're no jobs, no housing. Where would I go? I would go to my mother's house, where already three of my sisters and brothers are living. Is she going to look after me? That's quite a burden on her. She's 72, she has a heart condition. I'm an adult, I should be able to look after myself. I tell these [welfare] people, "I'm trying my best. I'm trying my best to stay out here and be an independent person, and do the best that I can." I have skills, I'm not stupid. I'm a half intelligent person here, and it doesn't seem to matter. I did a lot of government training programs. As far as I'm concerned there's a lot of Mickey Mouse programs. There's no job out there to meet my training.

I had problems up at the [social services] office. The girl at the front desk was very rude to me, but the next person she was very nice to. I said I don't have to be treated like that. I've learned through experience that I need to stop letting people talk to me like that. I spent my whole life with people calling me down, calling me names, and it's going to stop. To them I'm just a number, it has nothing to do with justice, it has nothing to do with helping your fellow human being. It's been more of a burden than a help. I don't take any pride in putting my hand out, asking for a handout. It's hard for me to even ask for help from my mother. I don't even know these people.

I tell them that I know five people without income, who are just sleeping on everybody else's couches. They are at the end of their rope. Well, we should appeal it. We can appeal it till the cows come home, the bottom line is [welfare] is not going to help.

You get so tired...

CHAPTER 4

Searching for Work at a Living Wage

I can tell what you are thinking,
Even beneath the phoney smile you wear:
Look at the fool pounding the pavement
With his papers
That show where he's been
But give no clue
To where he is going
You shake your head and say:
Sorry we're not hiring today
Then send me back out into the cold
Giving me not even another thought
Why should you, right?
Wake up!
This is the 90s.
The next time it could be you!!

Edgar

For most people living in poverty, the key to a better life is a job. Not just any job, but a job that pays enough to keep them out of poverty.

Although the employment situation in Ontario has gradually been improving since the last recession at the beginning of the 1990s, the jobless rate is still relatively high. (See Figure 6) Furthermore, while the restructuring of the economy has created new jobs, those jobs often require a very different set of skills than the jobs that have been eliminated by economic change. Many of the people who have been

Figure 6

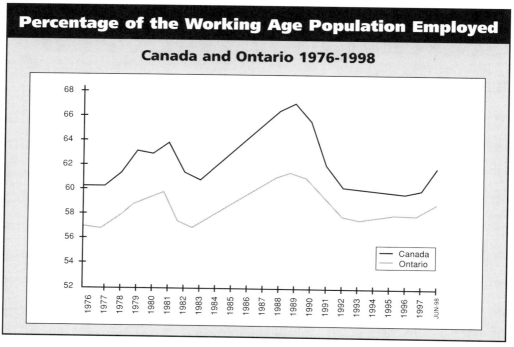

Percentage of the Working Age Population Employed

Canada and Ontario 1976-1998

forced out of the labour market by plant closures and business downsizings have a hard time finding work right away. And the longer people are out of work, the harder it is to get back into the workforce.

The percentage of employment that is part-time has been increasing steadily since the 1970s. (See Figure 7) It is much more difficult to make a living wage on part-time work. There is also more temporary or contract work available. Contract work may pay relatively well, but offers no income security.

In moderate-income families, the loss of a job by one of the parents can be a financial nightmare. Studies have shown that many Canadian families with children, living on a moderate income, are staying out of poverty only because both spouses are working in the paid labour force.

Working full-time does not necessarily mean a person can raise themselves out of poverty. As Figure 8 shows, working full-time at a minimum wage job leaves a single individual below the poverty line. If two people are being supported by one minimum wage job, or by two part-time minimum wage jobs, they are earning an income that is 58% of the poverty line.

A representative of the Peterborough Housing Advisory Committee, who spoke at our community meeting in that city, broke down income and expenses for a two-parent family of four earning one minimum wage:

Figure 7

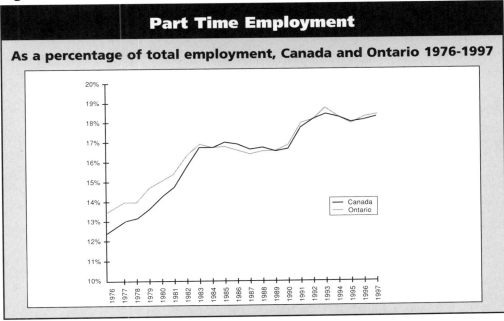

Part Time Employment

As a percentage of total employment, Canada and Ontario 1976-1997

Figure 8

Minimum Wages vs. the Poverty Line

Ontario 1996

**Sources: Canadian Council on Social Development, "Minimum wage rates in Canada, 1997."
Statistics Canada, Income Distributuins by size in Canada, Cat. 13-207-XPB**

Household Type	Poverty Line	Full time minimum wage earnings	Full time minimum wages earnings, as a percentage of poverty line
One person household	$17,132	$12,467	73%
Two person household	$21,414	$12,467	58%

Notes: Poverty line is the Statistics Canada Low Income cut-off (1992 base) for an urban area of population 500,000+. Full time minimum wages equals 35 hours per week for 52 weeks per year.

- income after deductions: less than $1,000 a month
- average market rent for a 3-bedroom unit: $747 a month
- food, clothes, utilities, transportation, entertainment, everything else: less than $300 a month

As of 1996, other income supports, such as the Child Tax Benefit, amounted to $267 a month, but many of them are not paid monthly, and thus may not be available to cover basic needs. As well, many people do not receive the supports because they do not file taxes, for reasons of language or literacy barriers, or for other reasons. Even if the same family has two minimum wages, their rent, a low-priced nutritious diet, and clothing would consume 65% of their income.

Job Hunting

Few things are more crucial to most people's dignity than the work they do. Many of those who spoke at the hearings told of the pride they took in the work they used to do and how it helped to define their sense of themselves as a contributing member of society. In the story that follows, a woman speaks longingly of her "other life" before she became poor.

In my case, you know, my other life, as I refer to it, is really not too far away and so it still hurts. You know, it's not too, too many years since I had another life. So I am fairly well dressed. I drive a good car, with air conditioning, no less, but right now I am poor. I am one of the so-called new poor, who at one time enjoyed all the trappings of being in the upper middle class. I used to live in a nice neighbourhood. In fact, I lived there for close to twenty years. I've held very good jobs. I was a town councillor. I was involved in everything going. I was really a leader, and I had a high profile in my community.

Now, unfortunately, that's all gone. I have been unemployed for two years. Right now, I have no house, not even an apartment. I have been forced to go back and live with relatives. I still have good clothes, thank God, hanging in my closet, a fairly good car to drive and I try as much as possible to move in the same circles as I did before.

Very few women who separate or divorce and remain single, can maintain the same lifestyle as before. Automatically, when I separated, I was pushed down into a lower socio-economic level. So in the late eighties, I chose to separate after 22 years of marriage. It was a decision that should have been made earlier, but my religious and moral upbringing prevented me from doing so. Eventually, my safety and my mental health outweighed the financial security, so I separated. And actually it was the best decision for all of us concerned. I have never looked back. Now, I am much, much happier, but poor.

So in the eighties there were jobs to be had. I had a number of contract positions and I could fall back on supply teaching. But that is not the situation anymore. When I moved back here last year, the first thing I did was walk into the school board offices. The supply list had been frozen since, I believe, 1991. I couldn't even supply. It wasn't even available any more.

Angela

I wanted to get a job, they tell you to go get a job, and I was trying my hardest, and it didn't happen. You just feel like you're maybe two inches high, and you know, you try your hardest to do what's right, and meanwhile you're not sure that there's a living for you and for your kids. I wasn't having a good time, but, I think we have to go through these areas in order to get stronger. I've gotten a lot stronger inside, just going through all these rough times. I was married, I had a divorce. I didn't want it, it happened.

I'm just going to mention that I go to the YMCA, and that's my

So I am fairly well dressed. I drive a good car, with air conditioning, no less, but right now I am poor. I am one of the so-called new poor, who at one time enjoyed all the trappings of being in the upper middle class.

outlet. I have to go, I have to get that stress out, not just because of the kids, but because of the financial problems of having to [get by on welfare], with the cost of things. The YMCA will never turn anybody away.

I know that with the stress of trying to find a job, there's a lot of stress in a lot of families, especially for the kids. The way that I became positive was because there was a group that was called Mothers and Others Making Change. I don't know if you've ever heard of it. [They were] positive people. You know, you get that positive feeling inside, and then you have that positive outlook on things.

My kids have to be looking for a future, and I don't really want to see them growing up [in a province] the way things are now. So I'd very much like to focus on the children in this society. Let's get this crying out of the way, let's see what these kids of ours can do. That's one thing. Another thing is we should be looking after the recycling, the world…

Don

Many of the people who spoke had gone to great lengths to take training, to get job experience, to do volunteer work to help themselves get out of poverty, but they were having a tough time. Some felt they were disadvantaged in the job market because of discrimination; some struggled with disabilities that, as one speaker explains below "do not show", but prevent them from working full-time.

I arrived in Canada as a refugee claimant in 1983, as a 19-year-old with a baby. I am from El Salvador. I had no right to work, nor to study English. To get per-

My kids have to be looking for a future, and I don't really want to see them growing up [in a province] the way things are now. So I'd very much like to focus on the children in this society.

mission to work, I needed to obtain a letter of an offer to work from an employer. I went to a restaurant, where the owners said I could start working right away. They would give me the letter later. I worked for a month, but never got the letter, nor did they ever pay me. The same happened in a cleaning job I got.

It took me a long time, and I had to get a lot of help just to get on social assistance at that time. Later, I got married and had two more kids, but it didn't work out, and we divorced. Eventually, I studied general business in a community college. After graduating, it was difficult for me to get work, but I finally found a job at a clothing store. There, I had to have very expensive clothes just to work, a different wardrobe for each season. The clothing was so expensive that I could hardly keep up with the other costs of living and raising three children, so I quit the job.

I thought it would be helpful to take some more courses, so I enrolled in a business school. This was a grave error. Once in the class, I realized that it wasn't anything like the quality of the community college's courses. I had taken a Ontario Student Assistance loan of $1,500 to pay for the course, and I tried to get the fee back, but they wouldn't return it. It was robbery! After the course, I applied for interest relief for the loan, since I didn't have a job right away, but the bank made a mistake which they didn't let me know about until too late, and in the end, I received no relief.

I couldn't make the payments, and the interest kept mounting. I finished school after the cuts to welfare [in 1995], and it was very difficult to survive. Before the cuts, I might have been able to pay off my loan while on assistance, by making a lot of sacrifices. After, it was impossible. Finally, someone told me that I could declare bankruptcy. I decided to do it. It feels horrible because I feel like I've done something criminal.

During school, the employment equity program was cut, which gave minorities support in obtaining employment. This program would have helped me a lot, because I have found that often I'm passed over for jobs just because of my name. I have seen people hired for jobs that I am much better qualified for. I find a lot of racism in Canadian society, especially quiet racism. People don't say anything, but you feel as if some people don't treat you as an equal.

The minimum wage here is ridiculous. It's a pittance when you're raising three kids. I worked for a while at a cafe where they pay by contract, so they don't have to pay employment insurance, Canada Pension, and other payments. They pay $6 an hour, and they only keep people on for three months, because after that workers are allowed to make complaints to the government. So they get rid of people before they can make complaints.

There are many companies doing this. Once, my boss there asked me to get up on a chair to get some ice off the front of the store. I said I wouldn't do that, because if something happened to me, I wouldn't be covered by Workers' Compensation. She got very upset about that. It seems I'll have a hard time keeping a lot of jobs because I won't put up with being treated wrongly. I come from a country where we had a war because of injustice, so how can I accept it here? I've been years without finding good work, and I know I'm a good worker. It feels like no matter how much I try to get up, there's always something that pushes me back down.

It has been very difficult for me in the last months. I try to keep busy, with various kinds of volunteer work. Even with that though, I find myself losing confidence that I can do work that I know I'm well qualified for.

It has been very difficult for me in the last months. I try to keep busy, with various kinds of volunteer work. Even with that though, I find myself losing confidence that I can do work that I know I'm well qualified for. I'm glad that the volunteer position that I have now, which I set up myself through the People Working and Learning program, is at a place where people are encouraging.

Rosalia

There are people in the community with disabilities that do not show. I'm one of those people, and I've found… in the last seven years, I've kept losing jobs. At present, I have been off work for a few months. I understand under our unemployment criteria, you must look for work, regardless of health. They don't care if we are suffering. I deliver papers two days a week. I applied to have medical papers signed a month ago because I'm a person who suffers from stress, anxiety and depression, and they said at Unemployment that they didn't know whether I would stay on regular benefits or sick benefits. They didn't have a clue. In the meantime, I must look for work, which I am doing every day. I get the interviews, but no jobs. I feel I am discriminated against because of my age. All we're asking for is to be heard and be employed. Okay, if we're supposed to get out and work, let them have jobs for us.

Carrie

Working on Welfare vs. Workfare

There seems to be a widespread assumption that people who are receiving welfare move on to the system for good, as a chosen lifestyle. The people who came to tell their stories made it clear that most recipients apply for welfare reluctantly and want to get out of the system as soon as they can. Statistics confirm that there is considerable movement in the system; most people do not stay on welfare indefinitely. On average, a single employable person receives welfare for a year and a half, and sole-support parent for 58 months.[1]

The line between the working poor and those on social assistance is fluid. Some people who work full-time receive a top-up from welfare. Sometimes the major benefit they receive is the drug card, plus a few dollars a month. The drug card is provided to welfare recipients to cover prescription medicines.

The issues related to employment for welfare recipients include more than just finding a job. On such a limited income, it is a struggle to set aside enough money for transportation to go to job interviews, a phone to be able to call prospective employers, and clothes to wear to work. For sole-support parents, a major issue is quality child care. Parents of young children also face the difficulty of finding work where the schedule does not interfere with parenting. As a sole-support mother's group from London wrote: "Single mothers wanting to work part-time cannot get jobs because of the shifts involved. Part-timers get mostly bad shifts. Since part-time work has terrible shifts and the minimum wage is $6.85 per hour and you must pay $5 an hour for babysitting, working becomes unbearable or impossible."

There are welfare recipients who work in the paid labour force. If they are in the Support to Employment Program or STEP, they can keep part of their earned income. The purpose is to encourage them to move to financial independence through work experience. STEP was one of the few reforms implemented among the many recommendations made by the Social Assistance Review Committee in 1988. Recent changes that the government has made to the STEP program mean that participants will be allowed to keep less and less of their earnings on a sliding scale that starts at 20% (reduced from the 25% described in the next story) and goes down to zero over a period of five years. Albert comments:

---

[1] Ontario Ministry of Community and Social Services, Statistics and Analysis Unit, fax, January, 1998.

The STEP program recognizes a person may be disabled and not be able to work-full time and fully support him/herself. However, they may be able to work part-time, enjoy going to school, or do meaningful volunteer activities in the community.

The first $160 I earn I keep without deductions from [my Family Benefits cheque]. After this I keep 25% of my work earnings. When 75% of my earned work income reaches the maximum amount I can receive from Family Benefits, I can no longer qualify for the [welfare] program. Depending upon the rent you pay, a person is able to earn between $950 and $1,360 a month without being cut off Family Benefits. People can receive no money from Family Benefits but keep the drug and dental plan. They have the security of knowing if their job becomes too stressful, if their place of employment closes down, they can once again receive Family Benefits.

Disabled persons can go off the program and attempt regular employment in the community. Because they can earn significant money while on the Family Benefits program, the transition to full employment is less difficult. If they find that they can not maintain full employment, they can return within one year to Family Benefits without having to reapply or without penalty.

Now, for my attempt at a career change, I had to build up my self-esteem that I could handle it. And so I had a number of volunteer experiences. I volunteered as an assistant to the chaplain at [a local agency], and that was a positive experience for me. And after that I moved, and I volunteered with [another local group] which is a psycho-social rehabilitation program. I took on more responsibilities there. And after that, a part-time paid position came up with [a local] self-help group. I was able to move into that position.

I'm really glad for this program, and I hope to get off social services at some time, but I hope it can be of my choice, at a time I choose to want to get off. I believe people have to feel safe in order to take risks, and this maintenance income allows me to feel safe to take some risks with school and with jobs.

STEP, it should be noted, was designed as a voluntary program. A concern that surfaced in all the community hearings was the introduction of mandatory workfare, which will affect everyone in the Ontario Works program except people over age 65 and those who get a temporary deferral. Mothers with small children for whom there is no publicly-supported education available (i.e. junior kindergarten) qualify for a deferral until the child is in a pre-school program. Workfare does not apply to people in the Ontario Disability Support Program. Workfare participants must take training or perform community service or other work—or lose their benefits.

The people who spoke about workfare were afraid and offended. People are afraid for a variety of reasons. Some single moms are afraid about having to leave their chil-

dren in someone else's care. Some people are afraid of failing in whatever training or job placement they are required to take. Everyone is offended at the implication—that they would only take training or a job if they were forced to do so. As Violet asked in the Owen Sound community meeting: "Why can't people work for a living rather than working for benefits?"

Particularly affected by ongoing changes in the job market are those on the margins—for example, people who have been out of the job market for a few years raising a family, young people just entering the job market, or people

If the government could do one thing to improve my situation, it should take away my fear of not being able to fend for myself. Help me to work in the community in a way which I could direct myself, using my past and present experiences to help others.

who have disabilities. People who are disabled are not supposed to be in Ontario Works, but there are many people who have applied for a disability classification under the old programs and have been turned down. It is expected that it will become even more difficult to quality for the new disability program.

The International Covenant on Economic, Social and Cultural Rights recognizes the right to work, which includes the right of everyone to have the opportunity to gain a living by work which they freely choose. ISARC believes that Ontario Works violates the pledge Canada made when the national government signed this covenant on behalf of the whole country.

A broad-brush tactic like mandatory workfare does not take into consideration individuals' particular needs, such as people who are on the borderline between a disability allowance and general welfare. The story below illustrates this concern.

[If the government could do one thing to improve my situation, it should] take away my fear of not being able to fend for myself. Help me to work in the community in a way which I could direct myself, using my past and present experiences to help others, i.e. help neglected or abused children with school work. But make it so I am paid a disability cheque for my work instead of being forced to work in a situation where I couldn't keep up or end up being humiliated and treated as a burden to society. The first basic need a needy person has is to be acknowledged.

Lucy

It is not that people on welfare don't want training and work experience and other supports to employment. They do. But hey just don't want to coerced. And they want real jobs and real training that are appropriate to their skills and experience.

Unpaid Work

Although we conceive of work more often than not as something that brings in income, many other activities can be considered as work. A group of single mothers in London wrote that society should value the work that mothers do at home with their children: "We are not just sitting home on our rear ends. We are doing volunteer work, going to school, looking after babies, toddlers, preschoolers, trying to find work, doing part-time jobs."

Unpaid work of all sorts contributes in immeasurable ways to building our communities.

Many people living on low incomes told of the importance of volunteer work to them, whether they saw it as helping them to some day find paid employment, or as a way to stay involved in community life, especially if they couldn't foresee holding a paying job. Some spoke of how their volunteer work shows potential employers that they have made a stable commitment over an extended period of time. Others said they derived great satisfaction from their volunteer work and it keeps their job skills sharpened. Donna explains:

> I am a single female, a member of a visible minority group, and over the age of 45. For the first 27 years after graduating from high school, number one in a class of 23, I worked as a secretary in a local plant. Then the day came when I was called into my supervisor's office at 10:50 for a meeting and out the door at 11:00 a.m. (due to restructuring).
>
> I spent months pounding the pavement looking for a paying job daily for eight hours. This failed to produce any results. The only result was that I got so depressed, I left the house one morning intending to end it all. This was stopped by a friend of mine who managed to catch up with me. After spending 10 days in the hospital later for a medical problem, it was discovered I was diabetic. Another strike against me. Now I had to worry about where I was going to get the money for drugs, blood testing equipment, etc.
>
> Not knowing where to turn, I telephoned Social and Family Services to see if I could get on their drug plan. I didn't want any welfare, just a drug plan. Thankfully, I was assigned to a very caring caseworker. She came to visit me and told me that I should not be embarrassed that I needed help. She said that's what they are there for, and I had paid for it [through my taxes for many years]. She also made arrangements for me to meet with an employment counsellor.

Then I had two people who cared, who believed I was worth something besides dirt. My employment counsellor got me interested in tutoring.

During my high school and working years, I spent most of my leisure time as a volunteer. Since losing my job, I have added more organizations to my volunteer list. The most rewarding is my tutoring. It brought tears to my eyes recently when I sat and listened to a lady read me a basic dinosaur book. Two months before that, she couldn't read anything. I have also worked on my qualifications for jobs. I went back to community college and received a diploma for computer studies, graduating on the dean's list. I also took a 10-week desktop publishing course at a cost of over $4,000.

For assistance, I receive $257 per month. I give my father $200 per month for my shelter and food and all other necessities. With the remainder, I purchase my blood testing strips ($44 per month). This leaves me with $13 per month for incidentals. Not much is it? But do you know what, I am happier now with my little $13 than when I was working and making good money. (Incidentally, before the welfare cuts, I was receiving $314 per month.)

Yes, I can be reimbursed the $44 per month for the blood testing strips. However, I have my necessities, I manage to get places I wouldn't be able to afford to go to by volunteering for organizations who sponsor things I am interested in. I took the job-finding club and discovered that I was searching for a job in the wrong manner. I have now refined this and yes, I am receiving a few interviews, but unfortunately no job.

I feel that I will never get a job here. I have too many things against me: a) my age b) my gender c) my diabetes, and d) the unmentionable, racial discrimination. Until I was laid off from work, I had never experienced racial discrimination here. My one "safe haven", my church, where you are supposed to feel safe and happy, is where I experienced it. Now, of course, although I am too busy to dwell on it, I (rightly or wrongly) put racial discrimination down to one of the main reasons why I cannot find a job.

Yes, I am poor. Yes, I am on the system. Yes, to all the other stereotypes most people have about people on the system. However, one big difference, I refuse to sit down and bemoan my position. If I can't find a paying job, I will find volunteer jobs.

Workfare is supposed to include community service work. At risk of stating the obvious, volunteer work is not volunteer work when not voluntarily done. To take away people's ability to give freely is in itself demeaning.

Effective Supports

Throughout the hearings, it became apparent that people were asking for effective supports to increase their potential to find a job that would provide an adequate standard of living for themselves and their children.

Several had participated in job training programs, but found no job at the end of them. Others could not get access to the training they needed. Some sole-support mothers spoke of the financial hardship of trying to get a post-secondary degree to improve their long-term jobs prospects. However, student assistance loans eliminate welfare benefits and increase indebtedness.

A major study of social assistance recipients in Ontario in 1995 showed that recipients tended to consider general education and skills training the most important supports they needed to find paid work. In addition, sole support parents identified quality child care as a fundamental need in order to be able to take on regular employment.

The greatest obstacles that hinder people in gaining self-reliance—the availability of jobs and services such as child care—are not under the control of individuals, but society as a whole.

Gillian's Story

From my perspective, poverty is violence. It is traumatic. I don't care about the external shame, in terms of how this government, previous governments, governments coming up, and society at large view the poor. The poor also internalize it—that they're lazy, there are jobs out there and they are not finding them, they're not trying hard enough.

I am a sole support mother of two. I was in school from 1990-91 and had to leave due to a mental health crisis. When I emerged from that three years later, and attempted to return to school, I learned from Ontario Student Assistance (OSAP)/Canada Student Loans that I owed nearly $6,000 in interest even though hospital doctors wrote letters regarding my circumstances. Basically mental illness is not considered a permanent disability.

To get OSAP to accept my new application, I would have to pay the loan off. To do this I had to borrow from the bank. Fortunately my bank manager is very understanding and concerned about poverty and has helped me through all my hard times. I borrowed $6,000 from the bank to repay the loan, applied to OSAP, got approved, but they delayed sending me the eligibility forms until a day after my classes ended, which meant that technically I couldn't get OSAP.

I borrowed again. I have been playing catch-up ever since—going to classes without food, using the Daily Bread Food Bank every two or three weeks because I didn't have enough. I get four hundred dollars to pay for books for the entire year, less than half of what I need. So, needless to say, myself and a lot of other sole support parents on campus are not getting sufficient money under OSAP.

What angers me more is that I will graduate with quadruple the amount of debt than students without children. OSAP is now considered income [by Social Services, and is thus subtracted from benefits], which I see almost as a punishment when you are trying to gain some independence and control in your life.

One problem parents have, especially single parents looking for work, is finding day care. Trying to find a job between 9 and 5 where no overtime is required or where you're not required to work until 6 p.m. on Friday is incredibly difficult. I have been looking for years. I ended up as a nanny, but it only lasted a few weeks. I took the job on the premise that since I'm caring for someone else's children, they might better understand my needs for flexibility. Unfortunately that wasn't so. On two days a week they didn't come home until 9 p.m. Although I couldn't afford it, I had to find someone to babysit, and I still owe $70 for that.

Once my employer didn't come home until 10 p.m. My sitter couldn't come that day and my son stayed alone for three hours, while I talked with him on the phone so he wouldn't be terrified. That was the last straw for me. I thought no matter how important it is for me to work, I'm not going to have my children suffer emotionally because of it. I have to draw the line somewhere.

After I left that job, I began to identify how much of the shame of poverty I have internalized. I really began to see a lot of the external aspects of poverty. From my perspective, poverty is violence. It is traumatic. I don't care about the external shame, in terms of how this government, previous governments, governments coming up, and society at large view the poor. The poor also internalize it—that they're lazy, there are jobs out there and they are not finding them, they're not trying hard enough... It makes you feel hopeless, worthless, blaming yourself for the choices you've made.

I know another sole support mom who makes entirely different choices than me, though we both live in poverty. I went over to her house one day and she was rationing food. Her kids got very little on their plates and they couldn't get any more. She has accepted that and that is how she gets through. I still maintain that I want my kids to grow up in a type of community where they can ride their bikes around without problems. We lived in a really bad area at one point... I preferred to spend the extra two or three hundred dollars and be somewhere else. However, I remember sitting with my therapist and saying... 'is something wrong with me because I'm making these choices that could cause me more financial hardship when I'm already poor and there's my friend who's making these choices where she rations her food, and she's living in subsidized housing?'

There are systematic things there to keep me where I am. I've come to this conclusion: Why must I choose between being a parent and being in poverty? It shouldn't be a choice.

When I came to Toronto I started university, while staying in a shelter. We applied to Metro Housing and I was told that my application was on hold because they didn't believe the type of abuse I suffered. I was only allowed to stay at the shelter for a short period. At the end of six months I was faced with no Metro Housing and no place to go, so I ended up on the streets. I don't mean in a shelter, I mean on the streets. I stayed in telephone booths, donut shops, I found a priest who let me stay in a church for a few nights, I sent my son to friends in the States. I tried to get things together because I didn't want him to go through this. I spent five months on the street. I got housing, I worked two jobs to save money to pay last month's rent. I was sexually assaulted on the premises, the individual was charged and sentenced to 5 years.

Under the strain of the criminal court process, I began having memories of childhood abuse. I ended up in the psych system, and my son in Children's Aid. The hospital staff did not believe that memories can be recovered after so long, so I was misdiagnosed as manic depressive and placed on anti-psychotic medications, which screwed up my mind. During this entire period I was separated from my son. I started doing some research myself. Contact with friends from my childhood confirmed that I was abused.

I met someone in the hospital from a privileged background, whose experience is vastly different from mine, both in her interaction with the administration, and her experience with her children. She had a nanny who cared for them and brought them in. She and her advocate were taken more seriously than I was. I was my only advocate. Whenever I spoke up, or questioned the diagnosis, I got labelled resistant to medication, to therapy. After I got information that proved to me what I remembered really happened, I separated myself completely from them, wrote letters to university and to Women's Health Centres to get supports in my life and go back to school. Because of my experience I chose to study psychology.

I'm faced with a whole new set of barriers to keep me where I am, where I have been, and where I have been trying to get out from. The anger is so overwhelming. Because I've begun to acknowledge how much of the poverty philosophy I have internalized I can direct that anger more outside rather than turning it in on myself. This summer I started an organization on campus. After what I've gone through since my return to university, I've realized how many gaps there are, how many people on campus are in the same situation. We are trying to build supports, and if they work I hope that they can be duplicated elsewhere.

The responsibility of the empowered people, people with social and economic power, is to change the social circumstances, and the responsibility of the disempowered is to empower themselves internally, to throw away the chains, throw away the self-blame, and throw away the self-doubts. That's the most we can ask of each group.

CHAPTER 5

The Necessities of Life

I personally have seen the health of my family worsen. My family scrapes together the last of the cash in order to make do. The cost of food rises and income drops. No work means we are doing without.

Ian

I am president of a local housing authority, which is housing for low-income people. Under the present government in Ontario, we are afraid that with the cutbacks there may not be any more low-income affordable housing in the future—housing that is and always will be needed.

Anna Rose

Adequate shelter and food are absolute necessities of life. In Ontario, we seem to have become used to the fact that many of our neighbours are having to resort to emergency hostels because they are homeless. We also seem to have become used to the fact that many of our neighbours must go to food banks because they don't have enough to eat.

Figure 9 shows the use of shelters in Toronto from 1988 to 1996. The increase in the number of families using shelters is extraordinary. Toronto is not the only community in Ontario where there are homeless people. The problem is all over Ontario. We heard from volunteers and community workers from Hamilton, London, Peterborough and St. Catharines who run programs (such as Out of the Cold) for the homeless and who have seen major increases in the use of shelters, especially among young people and families.

Figure 9

Hostel System Use of Shelters per night by Hostel Type

Toronto, 1988-1996 (yearly average)
Source: Springer, J. H., J. H. Mars and Melissa Dennison,
"A Profile of the Homeless Population in Toronto."
Report prepared for the Homelessness Action Task Force, draft, June 1998

Hostel Type	Youth	Families	Single Women	Single Men	TOTAL
1986	170	700	226	1,018	2,114
1989	183	595	224	977	1,979
1990	199	517	214	972	1,902
1991	198	671	231	927	2,027
1992	201	930	225	912	2,268
1993	195	1,120	229	1,015	2,559
1994	257	1,081	242	1,072	2,652
1995	319	1,648	256	1,014	3,237
1996	329	1,457	246	1,124	3,136
Change 1998-1996	94%	108%	9%	10%	48%

The Canadian Association of Food Banks does an annual survey of food banks across the country. *HungerCount 1998* reported that 290,925 people were assisted by food banks in Ontario during March, 1998. Food banks are becoming a way of life for many poor people.

Social Housing

Both the federal and provincial governments are in the process of withdrawing support for social housing. The federal government is downloading to the Province, and the Province is passing responsibility down to municipalities. Social housing includes the traditional public housing and non-profit and co-op housing options for low-income Ontarians. In addition, the Province has reduced the shelter allowances for people living on welfare. Together, these actions have:

- reduced housing options for low-income people and lengthened waiting lists for existing social housing;
- forced more low-income people to seek housing on the commercial market.
- resulted in many welfare families having to move out of the market-rate accommodation they were living in because they could no longer afford the rent;
- increased the use of emergency hostels.

The Province's decision to defund social housing projects in 1995 halted projects that had been in the works for five years in some communities. A representative from Niagara Peninsula Homes said the waiting list for social housing in the region is 1,500 deep, and low-income people are paying up to 75% of their income for housing in the commercial market. A spokesman for the disability community in Kitchener-Waterloo said the waiting list for handicapped-accessible accommodation for the physically disabled is more than five years' long. With no new units being built, the wait will only get longer. In London, the social housing waiting list has more than tripled since 1995.

The transfer of social housing to municipalities threatens the future of social housing because municipalities have a much smaller tax base on which to raise funds for housing, especially for people with special needs.

The transfer of social housing to municipalities threatens the future of social housing because municipalities have a much smaller tax base on which to raise funds for housing, especially for people with special needs. A panelist at the community hearing in Owen Sound described the probable effect of downloading on rural municipalities:

> Affordable housing is the number one concrete need. Fragmentation and lack of clarity as to areas of responsibility are a problem for everyone as services go to a municipal level in the midst of a rural area. For example, the reality is that mentally challenged and elderly people from the rural municipalities look to the towns for housing and services. Rural municipalities have no plans to provide these; towns don't want to provide them to non-residents.

Rent-geared-to-income housing can take several forms. The traditional public housing complex provides housing to low-income residents only. Speakers at the hearings called attention to two disadvantages of these developments:

- If a resident's income rises above the line that allows for subsidy, the renter must move out and find a new home.
- Large public housing complexes create whole neighbourhoods of poor people.

Public funding for affordable housing in the 1980s began to be directed more to mixed-income housing developments, with some market-level rental units and some rent-geared-to-income units. In these developments, once a family's income exceeds

Advocates for the physically disabled stressed the need for supports for their particular needs, especially around attendant care to allow independent living.

the subsidy limit, they don't have to move out; they just start paying a higher rent. The mixed-income developments also avoid the problem of creating housing complexes where only poor people live. Co-ops have been an increasingly popular form of non-profit housing that requires residents to work together to run their own housing development.

Judging by how often concerns were expressed in the hearings, there is widespread concern about the future of rental housing which offers low-income people a chance to have a decent place to live. Alana explains: "From what I understand, [the government] is trying to get rid of non-profit housing. For people on low-income, if that happens, I don't know what we're going to do."

Considerable concern was expressed about the future of affordable housing for people with special needs, including the physically disabled and people with mental health concerns. As one resident of a non-profit housing unit in St. Catharines said: "For the first time, I had a place that I could get some security. I didn't have to fear that someone was going to move out [of a shared tenancy] and I would be left without a place to live... People need safety in order to take risks." A representative of the Peterborough chapter of the Schizophrenia Society of Ontario said:

> The downloading to municipalities of the responsibility for social housing puts [the] whole concept of supportive dedicated housing for those with schizophrenia at risk. The behaviour manifested with a psychotic episode often contributes to evictions and black-listing of those with schizophrenia within both the market value and some rent-geared-to-income housing.

Esther told the hearing: "If I were to lose my CMHA (Canadian Mental Health Association) lodgings I would be out on the street—homeless. I cannot just live anywhere. I have specialized housing needs." Alexander expressed similar concerns: "I have known many mentally ill people and their needs. For those people, and myself, the idea of losing accommodations or never being able to get accommodations... could keep me from being as well as I can be."

Advocates for the physically disabled stressed the need for supports for their particular needs, especially around attendant care to allow independent living.

Many people with disabilities will need specialized housing for the rest of their lives.

For others, social housing may be only a temporary need. For example, women who have fled with their children from an abusive home often need housing for several months while they sort their lives and their finances out. Having an affordable place to live gives people the stability they need to knit their lives back together after a crisis.

Market Rent Housing

Contrary to popular belief, the vast majority of recipients of social assistance live in market rent housing. Although it is widely believed that most people receiving social assistance live in subsidized housing, Ministry of Community and Social Services information showed that in March 1994 only about 10% of recipients did. Fully 72% lived in private market rental housing; 7% were roomers or boarders; 7% were homeowners; and the remaining 4% were not identified, presumably including the homeless.

When poor people have to pay more in rent than they can really afford, what "gives" is the budget for everything else, especially food. Time and again, the community hearings were told that people are using food banks because they use up so much of their meagre incomes on housing. This has been a major factor in the rise of food banks over the last 15 years. A panel member in Peterborough wrote: "I was… made aware of the high cost of housing in Peterborough, and how little people on fixed incomes have left over for their needs. This high cost is at the root of the increasing situation of hunger in our city."

When poor people have to pay more in rent than they can really afford, what "gives" is the budget for everything else, especially food.

One presenter in Peterborough spoke of a young man he knows whose Employment Insurance benefits recently ended and who now receives social assistance. His rent is $420 per month and he receives $520 each month.

Average market rents for a one-bedroom apartment are far higher than the money allotted for shelter virtually everywhere in the province. In bigger cities, especially Toronto, rents within the maximum shelter allowance are almost impossible to find. Families in receipt of social assistance are in a slightly better position in smaller centres of the province because the rents are not as high as in the major cities. Nevertheless, their budgets are extremely limited.

Figure 10, on page 74, compares social assistance shelter benefits to average rents in centres around Ontario.

Utilities present an added burden. They are supposed be covered by the shelter allowance. If not, the money must be found elsewhere. A long, cold winter season can be a major problem for people trying to keep up with utility bills.

Figure 10

Social Assistance Shelter Benefits vs. Average Rents

Ontario Census Metropolitan Areas, October 1997
Source: Canada Mortgage and Housing Company

	Average Rent			
	Bachelor	One Bedroom	Two Bedroom	Three+ Bedroom
CMA	$405	$520	$636	$808
Hamilton	$409	$538	$630	$743
Kitchener	$406	$511	$636	$796
London	$515	$604	$691	$788
Oshawa	$483	$603	$729	$888
St. Catherines-Niagra	$374	$502	$613	$700
Sudbury	$388	$508	$619	$685
Thunder Bay	$385	$526	$666	$822
Toronto	$555	$685	$821	$975
Windsor	$400	$561	$680	$702
	One Person	Two Person	Three Person	Four Person
Maximum Shelter Allowance	$325	$511	$554	$602

Bill, an advocate for the disabled in Kitchener, underlined another obstacle all renters may soon face, whether low income or not—elimination of rent control for new tenants moving into a dwelling: "Rent increases have exceeded 2%. Elimination of rent controls will raise rents to a level our [the disabled] community is unable to pay. Once again we will be destitute and out on the streets."

A representative of the Metro Tenants' Association in Toronto said that court statistics show a 38% increase in evictions over the last couple of years. He considered this a low estimate since most people do not contest eviction and so do not show up as a court statistic. When told to leave, they leave. The power is in the landlord's hands, especially since most individuals are not aware of their rights as tenants. The low vacancy rate in Toronto reduces the ability of low-income renters to manoeuvre. The spokesman explained that a healthy vacancy rate is generally considered to be around 3%, but in Toronto the rate has been at or slightly above 1% for quite some time.

For one man, who is trying to take back control of his life, rent money is a major obstacle:

I just graduated from an Alcoholism Treatment Centre. I'm from the Chatham area, I'm 8 1/2 months sober. I'm extremely grateful for treatment, and I'm grateful to be alive. This is the first welfare I've ever received. I'm getting community start-up, welfare assistance, on my graduation. I was fortunate enough, a week ago, to find a sublet at $200/month. I managed to scrape up a $200 deposit. I don't have any money. Through working with counsellors and the centre, they lent me $200 to come up with my first month's rent, until welfare comes through.

I don't have any money, and I owe $200, and I guess I just wanted to share, because I have a fear of being homeless. My understanding is that addiction treatment centres have been taken out of the welfare system and moved over to Ministry of Health so they can say they cut welfare and spent more on health. So, now, as I graduate from the Ministry of Health, I'm having a hell of a time getting welfare. Like, I have to borrow money to get housing.

Something's wrong with the system. I'm doing a job search right now. That's kind of difficult too. I go over to [the mall], looking for a Canada Employment job kiosk, and I have to walk past 15 lottery booths before I find an out–of–order job kiosk, right. And I'm a little bit angry, frustrated, and I'm working my ass off to stay sober. I have lots of skills, and I want to be a tax-paying citizen, but I'm scared and you know, the opportunities just aren't there as they were at one time.

After my graduation—bottom line, I'm on the street—I'm out of the treatment centre, I'm on the street. It's up to me, I've been living for 8 1/2 months on a $25 a week comfort allowance, which isn't a lot of money to save first and last month's rent. And I'm sure you're aware that alcoholism is a disease. I thank you for keeping an open mind.

Jerry

Going Hungry

More and more people's cupboards are going bare from time to time, or even regularly. Jocelyn explains:

Je suis sans famille. Je dois dépendre d'une amie pour qu'elle me prête l'argent. Je suis constamment a la recherche d'un emploi, mais puisque je n'ai pas assez de nourriture ma santé en souffre et j'ai de la difficulté à me trouver un emploi. (I have no family. I am forced to depend on a friend to lend me money. I am constantly searching for a job, but my health is suffering from lack of food. It's hard to find work.")

Jocelyn

Many people in Ontario are going hungry. The reason they are going hungry is that they don't have enough money to buy nourishing food. The reduction in welfare benefits for many recipients has affected how much money is left over for food after rents and utilities are paid for the month. The declining purchasing power of a minimum wage has made it more difficult for families to cover all of their costs all of the time.

The Peterborough Social Planning Council reported on hunger in that city at the end of 1996. Through interviews in 138 low-income households, researchers found that 87% of the households had experienced some form of food insecurity during the previous year, ranging from anxiety about whether they would have enough money to buy food to going hungry for a day or more. Lack of income presented the most important barrier to food security. The report expressly uses the term "food security" in order to include more than hunger. The four dimensions of food security are:

Food banks have been providing a valuable service to the hungry for many years. But the people who run food banks are very aware that they do not provide an acceptable long-term response to hunger.

- a sufficient quantity of food;
- food that is safe and nutritious;
- food choices that are personally acceptable; and
- food acquired in a manner which ensures dignity and self-respect.

One-third of the households in the study had some employment earnings, while two-thirds received some form of government transfer payment, including employment insurance, workers' compensation or social assistance. Of those with employment earnings, over half received no money at all from the government.

Fifty-nine per cent in the survey thought that the best solution to the food problem they had faced or were facing would be a job or a better-paying job than they had; 16% saw lower-cost housing or utilities as their best solution, and a further 14% considered higher social assistance benefits the most effective way for them to meet their food needs.

The Peterborough hearing also heard about a local survey that the Peterborough County-City Health Unit did in June 1996 on the cost of a low-priced nutritious diet for a family of four. It came up with the figure of $127.28 per week, or $550 per month. This amount almost equals the entire basic allowance of $602 for a family of four on a social assistance income, leaving little for any other living costs.

Fighting Hunger

Food banks have been providing a valuable service to the hungry for many years. But the people who run food banks are very aware that they do not provide an acceptable long-term response to hunger. They consistently call for stronger measures to eliminate hunger from society. A report from Toronto's Daily Bread Food Bank concluded that: "in spite of their heroic efforts, food banks are an inappropriate way to ensure that the people of Ontario are fed; if food banks are to be categorized as 'private welfare systems' then it is clear that they cannot provide the security that even the sorely diminished government programs do."

People have come up with some innovative ideas to help fight hunger among low-income families. These include the Good Food Box, community kitchens, and community gardens.

Several people involved in Good Food Box programs across the province spoke at the hearings. Using the power of collective purchasing, Good Food Box programs provide a monthly supply of fresh vegetables and fruits for less than the retail cost. An organizer with Owen Sound FoodShare described their project as follows:

> We packed the Good Food box yesterday. We packed 230 boxes with food that people had paid for, and we still have money in the bank. And these are people who are not considered to have much consumer power, and now people are competing for our business, to be the suppliers for the Good Food Box. Together, we have consumer power, and in this society this means everything.

Alan, a promoter of the Good Food Box in the Niagara Peninsula, said organizers in that area attempt to find as much produce as possible from the local area and they have now begun to assemble dry goods boxes as well.

Community kitchens were mentioned by people in many different communities. The kitchens bring people together to cook a meal, divide it up into portions to take home, and use for several days. This way people can save money as well as enjoy the camaraderie of cooking together. For some, community kitchens offer a way to learn new skills in the kitchen.

Community gardens are another popular idea in many cities around the province. Land is made available either by local governments or private landowners, and is divided up into plots for individuals or families. In addition to being less expensive, the food is better tasting and often more nutritious than bought food. There is also the pleasure and satisfaction of watching the garden grow.

Eliminating Hunger

The Peterborough Food Access Workshop and Fair, held in March 1996 looked at wider questions of why people lack food security in the first place. Sponsored by the Peterborough Food Policy Action Coalition, the fair brought together local food producers, food access workers, and the public. The resolutions that emerged from this meeting included the following.

- Governments should recognize food security as a major health issue.
- There should be an integrated Food Security Strategy based on the right of all citizens to access affordable, nutritious, fresh, and safe food.
- Given the inadequacy of social assistance to meet basic nutritional health requirements, the basic living allowance should be increased to a standard that reflects today's cost-of-living in order for families to eat sufficiently and nutritiously.
- To ensure access to safe, nutritious food for the economically marginalized, strategies should be developed to ensure a fair wage, training for existing jobs, training and support for job creation, self-employment and community economic development.

These recommendations reflect the reality that more and better paid work and higher social assistance rates are keys to eliminating hunger in Ontario. All the other efforts are important either for their own sakes as good ways to make nutritious, local food available and affordable, or as temporary measures to address immediate hunger. But they do not offer the prospect of achieving the main goal: to eliminate hunger in Ontario.

Patricia's Story

I lived between my car and the 24 hour donut shop with three children for two weeks in February of 1996. There was no emergency housing or shelter for someone in my situation. I could not qualify for social assistance because I did not have a place to live [in that city].

I'd like to thank you for allowing me to share my story. I suffer from panic attacks, which can be very disabling at times. Someone unaware of these disorders has no understanding of the impact it has. If you don't have an apparent physical disability, you are not considered disabled.

I'd like to speak not just on my behalf, but on the behalf of others as well. This disorder has prevented me from leading a normal life. I'm unable to work, and have a difficult time going out. I am forced to depend on the [welfare] system. I have experienced hunger, homelessness and poverty. I have also experienced prejudice first hand, just for being poor.

When the cuts of 22% came into effect I was forced to move from a small town into the city. I rented a small place for myself and three children. When the owner found out I was on assistance, he refused to allow me to stay. He had accepted my money and allowed me to move my belongings in. Then he decided against it. He further stated he would charge me with trespassing if I stayed in the house.

I lived between my car and the 24 hour donut shop with three children for two weeks in February of 1996. There was no emergency housing or shelter for someone in my situation. I could not qualify for social assistance because I did not have a place to live [in that city]. The legal clinic helped recover my personal belongings. A landlord heard about the situation and offered me a place to live.

A friend told me about the food bank as I had no food for my children. She went in with me to help, as I have a difficult time in public situations. As I was getting some food, one of the workers started yelling at us—saying that we had just been in there and screaming at me to get out. I was so humiliated that I have not been back since. He realized after that he was mistaken. I still cannot go back. Many times I will live just on coffee or a bag of chips so that my children will have food. My son will go without eating or eat at friends' houses, so his younger sisters can have food. My younger daughter has special needs. She required hearing aids for both ears. It has taken two years to get them for her.

I don't think people realize what living like this does to a person. It's not just a matter of going without. It's what it does to a person emotionally, physically and spiritually. All sense of hope is taken away. You become oppressed and can no longer function. You suffer physically, because you are not eating, emotionally, because social contact is lost, spiritually because all hope is gone.

Day after day it wears you down to the point of giving up altogether. I thank God for the strength and the faith. Without it I would not have been able to cope with the difficulties I have faced. I am thankful for the fact of being able to keep my family together, and provide a warm and loving environment for them.

My hope is that people will become more understanding and compassionate of those less fortunate. That the attacks and blame on those who are poor will stop. Thank you for allowing me to share my story.

CHAPTER 6

The Health Factor

In the last year, the disabled community has experienced an increase in suicides. I personally know of seven who have chosen to end their pain, and one was my best friend. The community is fraught with depression, fear of loss of services, and intimidation from those who provide what we have left.

Bill

There is all sorts of research linking income and health. People who are poor are at risk of many more health problems than their more well-off neighbours.

Listening to the stories of our poorer neighbours, it is not hard to realize why. For one thing, being undernourished is not healthy. It is particularly damaging for growing children, and we heard many parents talk of going hungry themselves so that their children could have enough to eat.

People spoke of a vast array of issues related to health in their presentations. They spoke of how ill health prevented them from earning money, and conversely how not having enough money affected their health. People with physical disabilities and people with mental health concerns represented themselves strongly in many hearings, and outlined a stark picture of the challenges that their communities face in these times.

People spoke of going through debilitating levels of stress just trying to figure out how to survive and keep their families together on low incomes. They described how ongoing health problems interfered with their ability to work full-time or work at all. For some, a breakdown in health suddenly forced them out of a job and from a comfortable level of income on to hard times. The first story below describes how a workplace injury drove a young couple into poverty:

> While working on a construction site, Kerry was badly injured, and had to have his ankle rebuilt. As a result, he has a pronounced limp. He received worker's compensation for a while, topped up by welfare, but eventually his compensation ended. Janice and Kerry lost the home they were purchasing and had to go into public housing. They were grateful for low-income housing because they needed a decent place to raise their children.
>
> Janice has continued her schooling [from grade seven] through the years and has almost finished grade twelve. Kerry has two years of college and has taken various courses to improve his chances of getting employment. He has worked at several low-income jobs. Their son recently had to have expensive orthodontic work done and has a lot of expensive hardware in his mouth. Fortunately, Kerry's mother came through for them. The dentist said that their son would not even be able to eat if he didn't have the dental work done.
>
> With the cutbacks, Janice cannot feed her children the way they should eat according to Canada's Food Guide. She especially feels terrible when she has to deny them the proper amount of milk, in view of the state of her older son's teeth and jaw bone. The last job Kerry got had him flying sky high with happiness, dreaming of buying a home and breaking the welfare chain. After three weeks he was laid off because it was a security job, and someone decided that his limp would affect his work in an emergency.

Summary of Janice's presentation

I'm on welfare, I do odd jobs, but I'm physically unable to work an eight-hour job. Where I do work and where I volunteer I can work at my own pace and rest when I must, but my doctor does not feel I'm eligible for disability. I work harder than I should, but no matter what I do, I'll never get off welfare. You are not allowed to save any money which could eventually free you from the system. Every cent over $143 is deducted from my cheque.

Jennifer

Being out of a job in and of itself takes a toll on the health of many people. Being out of work for an extended period of time tends to affect people's physical and emotional health. For many people, work is health-sustaining. Having work is important for most people's self-esteem.

Health Care

Canada's public health care system protects all of us in many important ways. It ensures that people are not denied necessary health care services because they cannot afford to pay for them.

However, that does not mean that there are no income-related concerns about health care. The hearings were told that low-income earners who do not have drug benefit coverage at work or a drug card through welfare often choose not to treat illnesses simply because of the expense. People on social assistance have a drug card that covers many prescription medicines, but they still have to pay for whatever over-the-counter medicines they need.

There are also concerns—particularly among people with disabilities and people with mental health challenges—about availability and accessibility of health care services in communities across the province in the wake of restructuring in the system, including the closure of a number of hospitals.

As the following comments attest, for people suffering from serious conditions such as AIDS, many drug treatments are prohibitively expensive unless the medicine is covered by the provincial drug plan. And while a $2 dispensing fee doesn't sound like much to most people, it looms large for someone who has barely enough to live on.

> I am living with AIDS. And I am sick to death. I am not merely sick. I am sick to death about the inadequacy in our provincial drug plan, which means that many of my friends delay beginning possibly life-saving drug therapies because they cannot afford to fill the prescriptions. I am sick to death of a system that makes people decide whether to spend money on drugs or on food. I am sick to death that chronic and palliative care facilities in this region for those living with AIDS are woefully inadequate. A trusted friend told me recently about a man with advanced AIDS who could not find a placement in any chronic care facility in this region. Unable to cope, he killed himself. He died for lack of caring. And it just sickens me to death.
>
> **Dan**

> I live on a fixed income and have to budget carefully. Having to pay the drug store to fill my prescriptions can be a costly venture. Just imagine barely getting by financially and having to pay all those charges for your prescriptions, which can be numerous.
>
> **Alexander**

People with Disabilities

People with disabilities, and others close to them, formed a well-represented group at the hearings. Proportionately more disabled people live in poverty than the population at large. Given their special requirements for being able to participate in mainstream society, disabled people face a double barrier. Not only do they often have a more difficult time finding paid work, but they also have many costs that others don't. Wheelchairs, medications, transportation, and other aids and services increase the cost of living for many disabled people.

Although social assistance benefits have not been reduced for people with disabilities, other cuts have affected this group of people. For example, the fact that no more social housing is being built directly affects disabled people. The following comments sum up a range of concerns expressed by disabled people who are affected by service cuts and who have to get by on a low income:

> Life as a disabled person in Ontario and Canada is very bleak and the future looks even darker. We are forced to live with no future, no opportunity to get out six months of the year, fighting illness and depression. Our meagre incomes are being strained at every nook and cranny. If our support services have not been cut, they have greatly increased the cost of participation. We have no room to move, no funds to pay for anything else. We will soon have no choice but to live on the streets…
>
> Programs formerly covered by the regional governments under General Welfare funding such as repairs to assistive devices, like wheelchairs and walkers, are being reduced. Many municipalities no longer fund these repairs, nor dental work. Repairs are not covered by the Assistive Devices Program (ADP). Supplies like toilet seats, bath boards and shower seats are being eliminated from municipal and Home Care supply lists.
>
> These decisions are made regionally, which results in vast inequities across our province. This further strains the ability of the disabled to survive. The cuts to the health field are costing the disabled community dearly. The reduction of beds in hospitals, the possible closure of others, pose severe problems to the disabled. We have enough difficulty in accessing local hospitals and doctors as it is. If hospitals are going to close in the less populated areas, how are those of us with a disability going to receive hospital care? How can we even get there?
>
> The reduction of services relating to the disabled such as orthopaedic services is extremely important, as is physiotherapy. These are being taken away from us. We need these services just to keep our bodies supple and moveable. Without these we are going to have our joints and muscles seize. We will be further incapacitated. We are already disadvantaged, soon we will be discarded, to be forgotten, yet our pain will continue.

Bill

I depend on the health care system to stay alive. It costs money to keep me alive and so I get worried when dollars and cents seem to mean more than people. I worry that some bean counter in Toronto is going to say that it costs too much to keep me alive. There are countries in the world where this happens now— let's not become one of them.

Stacey

My name is Walter, and I'm a retired counsellor. I operate a very small agency—very small, because it's just me. I'm also a disabled pensioner. I'm on Canada Pension Disability, which is topped up by provincial disability. The Canada Pension Disability is indexed, so I get a raise every January, which is immediately taken off my provincial disability. Now, I'm getting into a complicated area here, but Canada Pension is taxable, the provincial pension is not taxable, so the bottom line is, every time I get a raise, I lose money. Now I'm no rocket scientist, but I know I can't afford any more raises.

Although social assistance benefits have not been reduced for people with disabilities, other cuts have affected this group of people.

I haven't had any increases in my pension in over four years, that's the length of time I've been on disability. My drug benefits—there's less and less of the medications that are covered by the drug card. Plus now there's a $2 dollar fee, so it really makes a difference.

I make the rounds of the churches because they have a lot of low-cost meals. It not only gives me the chance to save money, but it's also a time to socialize, and I think that's great. And I'm strictly non-denominational when it comes to a free dinner. I have not bought anything new for the last four years. And it's not all bad. The other day I bought a shirt I never would have bought even when I was working. Someone told me it was a $95 shirt, with just a wee hole in it. So, there's some up-sides to this too.

I can sort of struggle along, as long as nothing unforeseen comes up. The difficulty I have is when something happens to my old car. Most people on disability don't have cars. And this is something I've chosen to keep up because I have some serious breathing problems and we have some big hills here, so the car makes me much more mobile. So it's a thing that I really can't afford to have, but in a way I really can't afford not to.

I guess the poverty affects everybody in different ways. The overall feeling is

one of hopelessness, helplessness. It's a feeling that no matter what you do, how you budget, there's never going to be enough. And I'm always amazed at the end of every month that I've gotten through. When I've done the food banks, and all the other things, it's still really touch-and-go.

Now, working in the field, we worked for years and years to have low-income people treated with a little dignity. It seems to

I worry that some bean counter in Toronto is going to say that it costs too much to keep me alive. There are countries in the world where this happens now—let's not become one of them.

me that all the cuts have polarized the haves and the have-nots. There's an attitude out there that people on welfare are whiners, they're lazy, they're a part of some special interest group. I'm not quite sure what that group is. But it's the stigma attached. People are afraid to complain.

I worked last week with a lady with three young children, who had no food in the house whatsoever, and whose welfare cheque was late by 10 days for no apparent good reason. It was really panic city. I was able to get her some food on a very temporary basis. And the following day, they issued her cheque, and I took her up to get the cheque. Another of the problems is transportation. The welfare office isn't all that accessible. Because of all these cuts, and all this negative publicity about people on welfare, people are afraid now to speak out, because they might get cut off. And I can tell you that the people who are leaving the welfare rolls are not working, because the jobs are not out there. So, how they're surviving, I don't know. But that's the overall feeling for me. I've done hundreds of budgets for myself, and I still haven't figured out how to survive on this income.

Walter

The social assistance system recognizes that health plays a key factor in the ability of people to fend for themselves by giving increased levels of support to people who are disabled. Yet many people at the hearings noted that those with ongoing health problems do not necessarily receive disability benefits, even if they are entitled to them. These people must live on the general welfare rates for employable people, which are much lower than the disability allowance.

Different people ascribed their difficulties in being accepted for the disability allowance to different causes. Some felt their doctor did not take seriously their health problems. Others have doctors' reports that say they can't work, but their application is not accepted by the social assistance system. Clearly, many people face considerable obstacles in being accepted for disability allowance. A grey area separates disability from good health; any attempts to establish a clear line between the two will have arbitrary elements. Stories recounted at the hearings show that many people with serious health-related impediments to financial self-sufficiency are not receiving the benefits intended for people with disabilities:

> Andrea is 27, with three young boys, 6, 4, and 2. She collects family benefits. She recently has been diagnosed with a rare disease called *diabetes insipidus* or salt diabetes, the only case in Canada. Her mother's allowance did not cover the medications. The disease makes her shake a lot and slur her speech. Sometimes, she loses her balance when she walks. A few times she has even fallen down stairs. She may sometimes seem slightly intoxicated. The tremors in her hands make it difficult for her to hold things, even her children at times. For two years Andrea has tried to get on the disability program.

Summary of Andrea's presentation, Kitchener

> Jane has applied for Family Benefits Disability on the basis of manic depression and excruciating pain in her arm, pain so bad that she is unable to write her name. Her first application for disability was denied, but she didn't find out until one year later. Jane has tried using various types of medication including one which made her go bald. She has also sought to find a psychiatrist as well as specialists to diagnose the pain in her arm. Sleep deprivation caused by stress also plagues her. When her appeal to receive disability was rejected again, she was hospitalized in the psychiatric ward of a hospital because she was suicidal.

Summary of Jane's presentation

> Family Benefits have rejected my medical records as qualifying me, even though three doctors have said I am unemployable. I am mentally unfit to look for work now, and my doctor has certified this. If the government could do one thing to improve my situation, it would be to allow me to go on Family Benefits so I can at least live a low-income lifestyle.

Travis

With the new welfare legislation, the names of the benefits will change, but the distinction between benefits for disabled and for able-bodied people will remain.

However, there is a new definition of disability which is narrower than the old one. People who are currently on disability allowance are supposed to be transferred to the new program. However, many disabled people fear that the current eligibility review process will move some people off the old disability program before they have a chance to be transferred to the new one.

Mental Health

Each person who told of struggles related to mental health recounted a unique history. For some, mental illness prevents them from holding a job and supporting themselves. For others, the stress and anxiety of not having a job, and depending on an income insufficient for food, shelter, and other necessities, causes mental anguish and depression that can hurt more than the poverty they experience. Parents of growing children felt this especially sharply.

Many speakers in the hearings had been diagnosed with a mental illness that they have accepted, and that they expect to have to live with for a long time, if not the rest of their lives. Many of them were members of self-help groups that involve themselves with mental health issues.

The closure of psychiatric facilities was a major concern for many people. Those who need psychiatric care from time to time, and their relatives or friends, asked where the care would be delivered in their communities once a specialized psychiatric facility closed.

> Kathy was a public service worker until she became afflicted with depression and extreme fatigue. She attempted suicide twice and entered the psychiatric hospital twice. She feels supported by the programs of the hospital now and is concerned about the prospect of it closing without adequate supports put in its place.
>
> **Summary of Kathy's presentation**

Some of the saddest commentaries we heard were about people who are ready to give up on life:

> There has been an increase in diagnosis of depression, an increase in suicide attempts, a sense of hopelessness—many youth can't find a job despite their best efforts."
>
> **Youth Action Centre**

Recent public opinion in the last provincial election combined with drastic cuts to income have dashed many people's hopes, and demoralized people. I live in public housing, and I have a lot of friends through the shelter that I lived in,

through volunteer work, and so on, who are on social assistance, and I can really see the stress in their faces. I sat with a friend the other night who felt like committing suicide. She said, "What have I got left? I keep working and it's not getting any better. I try so hard."

We've had to kind of accompany each other a bit here and there. I try to fight feelings of hopelessness, and tell myself no, no, I have choices, I have choices. What are they, what are they? It's really hard, it becomes harder every day to go out there and look for that job."

Doris

Poverty's Impact on Health

A number of stories in other chapters talk about health problems among people who are impoverished. Poverty is stressful. It is not difficult to understand why people become desperate when they have been rejected over and over for jobs, they don't have enough money to feed their families well, and they have to worry constantly about emergencies using up the rent and food money. Poverty is especially hard to bear for people who have disabilities and for parents with children. It is inspiring how resilient and determined so many people are in the face of hardship.

Marilyn's Story

I **'ve had four years in university, I've got two degrees, $35,000 in debts, and no more closer to getting a job than four years ago. I'm about two inches away from [joining the sex trade]... I have no choice—my children are going to eat, or not eat.**

I'm from..., and we have a community with ultra-rich, who are having country estates built all over the place. At the same time, I was in a home a month ago, eating left-over chicken, the chicken that you would throw out, but they were refrying it the next day so you could suck on the bones and get calcium. This is the kind of chronic stuff that people are not opening their mouths about. They are so humiliated to be demeaned to such an extent, that they're never going to tell you about it. And so I'm here to tell you what they're telling me.

I know what hunger is like. I'm sick and tired of it. This is supposed to be a civil society, a liberal society. Why should there be anyone hungry in a First World country? I have a grand-daughter who was born with a withered hand, that's going to cost us $260 a month for the rest of this child's life. That was not genetics. It was extreme duress in the womb.

I've had four years in university, I've got two degrees, $35,000 in debts, and no more closer to getting a job than four years ago. I'm about two inches away from [joining the sex trade]... I have no choice—my children are going to eat, or not eat. And yet years ago, I preached the gospel of Jesus Christ. I ministered in Haiti, I taught my children at home, I spent five years doing home schooling. I'm not stupid. I'm not a slut, and I'm not ignorant. I'm really a dynamic member of the community, but I'm always shoved to the back. I can't get a job.

I have my own personal agenda with this. I refuse to go to the food bank. I refuse to be an object of benevolence. That's the way I feel about it. I've been so hungry... But I would rather die than eat the food that comes out of food banks. Number one, they're run by university people, not by the poor. Why do university graduates get pay cheques on poverty? My poverty creates a lot of jobs. Every time we take from a food bank, we're telling people that they're doing a wonderful job. People put their cans there, and they wipe off their hands, and say, God bless you, I've done my part. Well, they haven't. They haven't done their part until I get an apology from the Ontario government for the atrocities that they've committed against my family.

The reason we have poverty is because we create it. We're talking about globalization. People are shoving their money into mutual funds, and RRSPs and they're whipping the people in Third World countries. There's not just a unity among the poor in Canada, it's international. We were 20% before, but when you put it on a global level, we're 80% of the population.

We don't have to prove that we're not lazy. The studies have been done ad nauseum on who welfare people are, and where they're going, and what they want to do. But it does not count with the kind of mentality that's out there. And now, I think the thing that hurts the most is the fact that the churches didn't back us up.

I have never, never, had such a hard time in my life. The medications they give me, I'm classed as chronically depressed. And I said give me a job, and you'll see how unchronically depressed I'll get. So, my behaviour becomes pathologized, but not theirs... They've made it okay to use words like you welfare bums, you lazy cheats—now it's fashionable to be fascist again. That's just such a slap in the face.

And it's coming from every direction. I've known women in hospitals who were insulted—they said all you are is a welfare mom. You got knocked up in your teens, and who the hell do you think you are that we have to support you. The number of teen welfare moms is about 6% in Ontario, 2% nation-wide. So, there's a perception that all the single moms are a bunch of women that got pregnant in their teens. But most of them are women who have been separated, divorced. That is enough to go through, you don't need anything else. Or they are widows, like me.

The perception that is put around [is] deliberate. I wish I had a team of people to go into the newspapers, because I have noticed articles in the newspaper about welfare fraud that are blatantly dishonest. I wrote letters to the editor about it. Welfare fraud is still considered front-page material. And so I have to keep on writing them back, and saying, what about white and blue collar fraud?

If something doesn't change, people are going to commit suicide. That's the way it is, you just accept it. Malnourishment has created a number of health problems for me, and ultimately that will cost you. I've lost 75 pounds averaging a meal a day for a year and a half. If I have to lie, cheat, steal, I'm going to. I'm going to have to do something, because I'm frightened that by hanging around with women who have been forced into the sex trade, that's where I'm going to end up.

I can't allow people to walk over my boundaries any more. Telling me how to take care of my children anymore. We don't even have a home. We don't even sit at the same table and eat. I've got two teenage boys, I had to tell them there was no food. They were already eating leftovers from their friends' lunches at school. How many people in Canada have had to do that?

The pain is so deep. Every single day, I'm looking at people who are hungry, who are scrounging around, [to] get ten bucks together. What kind of society have we made, that takes a woman out of the pulpit, and puts her in the street?

But we're living in it—it's very real.

Everybody's using what I call the language of compliance—trying to keep people quiet and calm. They're not saying: Get up and get angry. Start doing. We've all got pens, we've all got paper. Write your articles, send them out. I never thought I could write, but I did.

CHAPTER 7

Moms and Kids

In my most vivid imagination, I could not have fathomed that my sons and I would be among the faces of poverty.

Cheryl

Many parents came to the Neighbour to Neighbour hearings around the province to tell their stories. Some were poor because they fled with young children from abusive relationships. Some were poor because they lost their jobs. Some, like Cheryl (above) were poor because the government system set up to ensure they received child support payments failed.

Some of the most poignant stories were told by mothers who were trying so hard to protect their children from the worst effects of impoverishment—hunger, shame, loss of opportunity.

This chapter includes stories from three different moms, talking about their kids— their kids' education, their kids' safety, their kids' health, their kids' future. Their circumstances are all different. Their love speaks for itself.

This government doesn't seem to realize that a relatively small amount of money spent now on these special needs children will show phenomenal growth over the years.

… My name is Gail, and I'm a single mom. I have been on social assistance in the past, and luckily I don't have to be anymore. But the reason I'm here to talk is for a very special reason to my heart—my children, specifically, my son, Aaron. He's eight years old and autistic. He was diagnosed approximately four years ago, thanks to a very wonderful teacher. Until that point I was told it was all in my head. But she realized there was a problem and had him identified and diagnosed and what not through the school. So began my challenges.

Now, raising a special needs child is very challenging, but not for the reasons that may seem obvious to you. The hardest thing about raising a child like Aaron is having to come to grips with the idea that, for very selfish reasons, I will never see my son get married, I will never have grandchildren by my son. But the hardest challenge I ever had to face was being told that my son would never fit into mainstream society, and not because he didn't have the potential to be educated, but because the services weren't there to educate him.

Autistic children are wonderful in that if they are given intense consistent training at a very young age, they develop, they flourish and they can actually become normal within a short period of time. Unfortunately, when Aaron was diagnosed, he had just fallen outside this range, this category, but there was still hope. So I fought, I advocated, and I tried my best to get him services. Then came Mike Harris.

First of all, my son, at that time, didn't speak. He had no language. Now, in the school system, speech is important. I went to special services at home and was granted some funding, and through that I got him speech therapy. I would go to a speech therapist, have her outline the program and get his special needs worker to then work through the program with him.

As of this year, special services at home has been frozen, which means that more and more children are being diagnosed, but there's no money there for the parents to get the services that they need for their children. And those services that haven't been frozen or cut are changing their mandate so that children like Aaron who suffer from a spectrum disorder [whose autism is not as severe] will no longer be served.

That means that families in [this] area are hit not once, not twice, but three times. They don't get respite. They don't get special services at home. They don't get the funds that are available for special foods that their children may need to eat or braces or wheelchairs or other mobility aids, in some cases. This has left the parents and the families frantic… I have seen teaching positions cut and eliminated. I have seen children who were somewhat ready for integration being thrown into classrooms. Previously, they were in a classroom with six children with a special worker and then they are thrust into a classroom of thirty children with the teacher not getting any assistance, nor the child, and the parents being told to deal with it, to offer the extras at home.

These children are being failed miserably by our education system, not because the teachers aren't caring, not because the teachers don't want to, but because there are no funds there. How do I explain to my child that he's not seen by the government as special enough to get the services that he needs?

It's ludicrous that we can't have qualified teachers because there isn't enough money. This government doesn't seem to realize that a relatively small amount of money spent now on these special needs children will show phenomenal growth over the years, and by the time they are adult age, they will rely less on welfare, on halfway houses, on all these other services. I get very emotional about this.

I guess what I'm trying to say is I'm hurt. I always believed that I was growing up in a country that valued its people, that valued its children, and that saw its children as a commodity for the future. Our children will lead the way tomorrow. But the underlying feeling I've gotten over the past two years is that the children who society should take care of the most—and I'm not talking just kids with special needs, I'm talking kids with emotional problems, kids who need attention—are the ones who are being left out the most. The government's attitude is, we'll take care of the so-called normal kids and they will be the social workers of tomorrow, they will take care of these kids and will deal with it then

Gail

I'm on Mother's Allowance, I have three boys. They're 11, 9, and 2, and I've come out to tell my story, why I'm on the system.

And basically, I don't think it should be a surprise to anybody. There are limited jobs, and when you're on your own, with three children, you are immediately in a different category. You haven't got anyone there. If you have a spouse or somebody else to help out with things, it takes a lot of the burden off, but I don't have that. Like I say, I'm up until 2 in the morning, and then up in the morning with the children to go to school, and then busy all day long. People say, "What do you do?" There's unlimited [things to do]. Otherwise I wouldn't be up until 2 in the morning.

There is a lot of fear. One day I sent my children to school, thinking the two are happy, the one's at home, and I get a phone call— "Your child's up at the hospital with a broken arm."

There is a lot of fear. One day I sent my children to school, thinking the two are happy, the one's at home, and I get a phone call—"Your child's up at the hospital with a broken arm." The whole time I was at the hospital I was thinking, "What would I have done if I was working?" Their father doesn't live in town, my mother works, my father doesn't live in [town]. All I have is me.

There's a lot of good people out there, a lot of people who are willing to help, but you feel like a burden. Raising good quality children is something. Whereas if I was working and had to leave them, I would need day care for one and some after-school care for the other two. I would hardly see them. I would come home and I would have so much to do that that the time would be gone. I still do have quality time with my children.

We are in a neighbourhood now, not by choice, but one that allows me an affordable home, and it's a struggle to keep my children on the straight and narrow. People don't realize, when you're living on a low income, there's so many things coming at you. I have friends who are happily married, they have children, they're working, and they don't have any of that. They're shocked because they're not exposed to it. At 11 years old, I shouldn't have to sit and monitor my kids playing outside but I do. So that they don't come home with things that I don't think they should know.

I think single parents need a lot, a lot of help and encouragement, and hand-holding if you will—it sounds silly—to get them back in there. When I have tried to take courses, I have had doors closed in my face. For instance, I wanted to take a course at community college for health care aide. It would have given me a reasonable job. But I was told, "We're not sure if you qualify for the bursary." The course was $700. That doesn't seem like much to some people, but for me, there was absolutely no way I could pay $700. I could apply for the bursary, but I wouldn't know if I got it until the course was halfway through. I was told if I didn't get it, I would have to pay then and there for the term. Well, who would be foolish enough to put yourself in that kind of a debt position? You're already low income. So of course I didn't take the course, and I find out the next year at income tax time that I did qualify for the bursary.

When people have been brought down to low income, it's a feeling of just wanting to sit down and close the door, forget it, not try for a bit, take a break.

Single parents need help... They're saying there's these training programs—there aren't. And what training programs there were, I found, once you were done, that the pay was so low, that you would be trapped again.

That's how you get stuck there. And when people just want to open the door and get a little bit of help and it's not there—that's it—people sit in their home, and I see that where I live, I see people who aren't willing to open the door any more, to go out.

Before the cuts, I had relocated to a [larger nearby city]. There was a lot of help there. They do have people coming into your home, but they are not intrusive. Here I find it's intrusive. I was renting a townhouse that wasn't government [public housing]. I had to move instantly, when we found out about the cutbacks. There was no way. I would have been left with $100 a month for food, bills, everything. The only option I had was to come back here, because there was a huge waiting list in that area for government housing. My children were in a good school. We were quite happy there, and I felt we would have been better off there. Bigger centre, more jobs, whereas in this area where I am now, all we see is single parents on low income.

With the cutbacks, we struggle every month just to eat. So where the attitude comes from that you're sitting around having a heyday– why anyone would want to sit there and make that kind of money—I really don't know.

Single parents should be categorized differently than people that are on their own. If I was on my own, there're all kinds of things I could do. I would do anything. Same thing with couples. Single parents need help... They're saying there're these training programs—there aren't. And what training programs there were, I found, once you were done, the pay was so low, that you would be trapped again. Once you're there, it's so hard to get out. It's like you're trying to jump up, and you're just about to the top, and then bang, back in.

Right now, I'm not sure what I'm going to do, because so many different things are coming at us so fast...like workfare. The other day I was watching a program about resumes, and I was interested and writing things down, thinking this is great information, and then a mother phoned in, and asked, "Well, I've been home taking care of my children, how do I put that down?" And he said, "Don't. That's the worst thing an employer can see." And I thought, there you go.

Eleanor

I am a single mother with one daughter. Immediately after her birth I returned to work as a Health Care Aide. The work was part-time with irregular hours. Though my earnings were not abundant, I managed to stretch them to meet our needs.

The first babysitter my daughter went to showed the children horror movies. After seeing a severed hand scrabble out of a toilet, and grab a small child by the neck, my two-year-old refused to go into the washroom. I can't say that I blame her. I moved my daughter to a day care centre. A short time later cutbacks forced them to reduce their hours. I had to move my daughter to someone who could accommodate my working hours. The next babysitter seemed ideal, until I found out my daughter was being molested. She refused to leave my side. I had no choice but to stay home and care for her myself.

When she started going to school full-time, I returned to school myself. I was unable to finish school because of arthritis. They don't like to perform knee replacements until a person is 60 years old. I was told to return when my knees become the size of basketballs and I can't walk anymore. After one of these operations, I would be laid up for several months, an impossible situation when you have a child. I was told to avoid kneeling, crouching, and climbing stairs. I walk with crutches to try to save my legs for as long as possible. I had to move out of my residence of eight years and into a smaller apartment with an elevator.

I also have fibromyalgia, a disease characterized by chronic pain, chronic fatigue, migraine headaches and cognitive problems including short-term memory loss, word mixups, mood swings, irritability and a loss of endurance. I have a list of aides and therapies that have been recommended. But custom shoes are $200 or more, knee braces are $40, Y memberships are $300, and a special light is $200. The list goes on. Welfare told me I was eligible for an increase due to my inability for work. I didn't ask for this, my case worker suggested it when she found out I had arthritis. I took the application papers to my doctor and he just laughed and told me I didn't need it.

I receive $615.48 per month, after I have paid my bills, bought groceries, and done laundry, I am left with approximately $50 per month. This $50 must pay for clothing, shoes, medicines, entertainment, birthday and Christmas gifts and all other household expenses. Custom shoes, etc. are out of the question. A bus pass costs $46 per month. One round trip costs $7 for the two of us. My world has shrunk to a three block radius.

Grocery shopping and household chores have become difficult, painful, and sometimes impossible. If I push myself and do more than I should, I end up in extreme pain, and am unable to perform even the most routine tasks. The more I overexert myself, the longer it takes to recover. The medical community has no cure for fibromyalgia, the arthritis will not go away, and I worry constantly about my future, physical and financial.

I live in fear, worrying that I may become ineligible for Mother's Allowance. I have been told by a social worker that when your child turns a certain age, you are expected to get a job. My daughter turns twelve in ten months. I don't know how I could ever obtain or keep a job.

My daughter is hyperactive and keeping her very busy was the best solution for us. At the age of three we spent many days hiking, going swimming at the Y and after supper she would want to return to the Y. By the age of nine we were biking 12 km. At ten we were biking 40 km. When she is active, she's happy. Her energy levels have risen, but mine have been lost. It is very difficult for her to make the adjustment. She is not old enough to do these things alone.

She has had to take on extra responsibilities around the house. She is a loving child who nurses me when I am having a bad day, bringing me cups of tea and heating pads. She is the one who carries the groceries, and gets down on her knees to scrub the floors. Like Cinderella, she has lost her good mother and is now living with an inadequate one. Her world has shrunk to the same three-block radius as mine.

I have many wonderful memories of my childhood. It breaks my heart to think of the memories she will have.

Alice

One of the hardest things for these mothers is to see the hardship of their lives affecting their children. In closing, here's a poem written by some children in North Bay. It is poverty from a child's point of view.

Poverty is...

Wishing you could go to McDonald's
getting a basket from the Santa Fund
feeling ashamed when my dad can't get a job
not buying books at the book fair
not getting to go to birthday parties
hearing my mom and dad fight over money
not ever getting a pet because it costs too much
wishing you had a nice house
not being able to go camping
not getting a hot dog on hot dog day
not getting pizza on pizza day
not going to Canada's Wonderland
not being able to have your friends sleep over
pretending that you forgot your lunch
being afraid to tell your mom that you need gym shoes
not having any breakfast sometimes
not being able to play hockey
sometimes really hard because my mom gets scared and she cries
hiding your feet so the teacher won't get cross when you don't have boots
not being able to go to Cubs or play soccer
not being able to take swimming lessons
not being able to take the electives at school (downhill skiing)
not being able to afford a holiday
not having pretty barrettes for your hair
not having your own private backyard
being teased for the way you are dressed
not getting to go on school trips

—Grade 4 & 5 children, North Bay

Louise's Story

The cuts to education mean that I have to find my own sources of testing and educational support for my children with learning problems. The charges for driver's licences and insurance mean that I will likely never drive, or have use of a vehicle again, and thus never be completely self-reliant. Cuts to municipal transfers have been passed down, so that there are changes now in the local transit times and fees. And this has meant that I can't get to the church of my choice, and must pay $18.50 round trip to go anywhere in town on the bus with my family.

My personal story is that I am the oldest child of a minister who worked professionally in social work and his wife who was a florist. Both have since retired. I have a degree in psychology, and have done some work towards a Master's. I'm sort of your middle-class kind of person. I'm also a survivor of an abusive marriage, and I have six children, two years to 13 years.

I am currently a recipient of social assistance and operate a barter club business. The cuts in welfare funding have placed an incredible strain on our budget. I can only pay the most immediate bills, falling constantly behind to pay for clothing, birthday presents, any kind of summer camp. Our food budget of $300 per month is restricted to things that are filling and cheap, like bread and pasta. Milk and meat have become luxuries. Vitamin pills have become a nutritional necessity.

The pressure on welfare to cut even further has spawned new regulations regarding small business operators, which makes it tremendously difficult to create employment for yourself. If you get a loan from someone, a bank or another person, it's deducted at value. You can't use social assistance funds to start up, to expand. You can't reinvest the money that you do earn without restrictions and you have to get permission.

I use my child tax credit for necessities like food and utilities. I'll be real depressed if they claw it back. My $673 shelter allowance doesn't cover the $700 I pay in rent, the $75 I pay for gas, and the $135 a month I pay for electricity. It all comes out of my food budget. Cuts to education have made it more expensive to send my daughters to school than it has been to home school my two oldest boys. Originally I home-schooled because the children had learning problems. It has become a concern now—about having no food in the house for their lunch, no money for field trips, no money to replace worn clothing.

The changes in the local busing have made the walk too far for my sons if they did want to go to school. Changes in the drug card mean that I fear illness, if we need a prescription for something that isn't on the card. Frequently I don't even have the $2 dispensing fee.

A feeling of hopelessness, of twisting in the wind, and getting nowhere is very strong. I love my children dearly, and it breaks my heart not to be able to provide as well as I'd like to for them. I'm lucky that I have an excellent network of support. I'm aware that a lot of other people do not.

The cuts to education mean that I have to find my own sources of testing and educational support for my children with learning problems. The charges for driver's licences and insurance mean that I will likely never drive, or have use of a vehicle again, and thus never be completely self-reliant. Cuts to municipal transfers have been passed down, so that there are changes now in the local transit times and fees. And this has meant that I can't get to the church of my choice, and must pay $18.50 round trip to go anywhere in town on the bus with my family.

That's my sad story, but I'm aware that the cuts really affect everyone somehow, and I know that my family is lucky not to be living on the street or worse. I appreciate the support I have received from this community which is why I volunteer and give back as much as I can, and why I'm here. One of the nice things about being part of a smaller Ontario community has been the way people look out for each other.

One of the worst effects of the cuts, to my mind, has been neighbour turning against neighbour. This government has encouraged us to focus on the boogey man amongst us, and away from its own hidden agendas and lack of foresight. Most people want to be employed or useful to society. They want adequate resources to take care of their families, and feel a sense of self-worth. They want to feel some security and reasonably good health.

We need to focus on what we have in common. I hope that this forum takes the sad stories and moves forward to find ways to facilitate the strengthening of community responses to what is happening. We need to work together and to support each other. We need to share and be pro-active in our community, to ensure that the resources we have are directed to keeping families whole and strong, to prevention, to healing, to helping all people reach their fullest potential.

CHAPTER 8

How Should We Respond?

We need to focus on what we have in common. I hope that this forum takes the sad stories and moves forward to find ways to facilitate the strengthening of community responses to what is happening. We need to work together and to support each other. We need to share and be pro-active in our community, to ensure that the resources we have are directed to keeping families whole and strong, to prevention, to healing, to helping all people reach their fullest potential.

From Louise's Story

We hope, as Louise has asked us, to take these "sad stories" and move forward to strengthen community responses to poverty, hunger and homelessness in Ontario. These stories are not just about individual suffering. They illustrate a serious division in our society. Poverty separates a significant segment of our community from the mainstream. This marginalization not only hurts those who are impoverished—it also diminishes our community.

It is important to emphasize, as well, that the poverty described in these stories is a systemic, not an individual, problem. Many of these people are poor because our economy is not producing enough good jobs. Some do not have access to appropriate education and training and employment-related support services, such as child care. Many of these people are poor because they can't work or they can't find work and the income support programs our governments provide are inadequate.

How do we move forward to strengthen community responses to poverty, hunger and homelessness? Consider these thoughtful observations from a leader of a faith community who attended one of the Neighbour to Neighbour hearings:

> In the fifteen years that I have been a priest, I have obviously been involved with a lot of people who are struggling in their lives in very many different ways. So it's not as if it is a discovery for me that there are people who are struggling. But for me this [Neighbour to Neighbour hearing] is the first time that I have participated in a situation where people have come together to tell stories and to listen to stories, and I think it's the cumulative impact of all of those stories that is really frightening for me.
>
> And one of the things that frightens me the most, I realized as I was listening to the stories this evening, is a conversation I had last night with a couple of friends of mine who are very good people. I was telling them that I was coming here and their first reaction was: "Well, don't get taken in now, because you'll hear a lot of really nice stories, you know, but most people aren't like that. Most of these people, they're out to cheat."
>
> The people who were saying this are good people. And this really frightens me. There is an attitude in our society today that people who are struggling deserve to be struggling and somehow have brought it on themselves and it is up to them to get out of their problems. That is so different from the experience that is mine from my parents, who speak to me of where they grew up and the poverty that they knew, but where there was always an extra place at the table for somebody who was poorer than them. In that sense, I think what we need to rediscover is community, and we need to rebuild, reweave a true sense of community in our country.
>
> Right now what scares me is the feeling that everybody's pulling on their end of the blanket, and the blanket is slowly being torn and some people are being left with fragments of that blanket.
>
> There was a powerful image for the early Christian writers of the first three, four centuries—that the poor were the sacrament of Christ, that when you met someone who was struggling with poverty somehow you were being faced with the very mystery that is at the foundation of our faith. I would say that today, as a leader of a Christian church, I must admit that very few members of my church live that, believe that, or know that, and I think that this [meeting] has been kind of a challenge to me as a leader in my church to work to change that and to rediscover the sense that we are all in this together and to rebuild community.

Msgr. Paul Andre Durocher,
Auxiliary Bishop, Diocese of Sault Ste. Marie

The comments from Msgr. Durocher capture wonderfully two themes that ISARC would like to emphasize:

- The misunderstanding among "good people" of how the less fortunate end up in poverty and in need, and what their lives are like.
- The need to repair and reknit the social safety net and rebuild our sense of community.

To move forward will require changes in public attitudes and changes in public policies. Each of us needs to take up the challenge both individually and as a member of the community.

As we stressed in the Introduction, as faith communities we accept our obligation to help our neighbours through charitable efforts. But charity is not enough. As Stephanie, a volunteer with the Out of the Cold program, which provides a safe place to sleep for the homeless in winter, has said:

> Government has said that the churches need to be doing more. Yes and no. Yes, we can provide food and shelter, friendship, support, volunteers, and education for volunteers. We can work with the agencies and support them through the cutbacks. But churches cannot provide help all year-round. We have neither the resources nor the energy. We cannot provide for day-to-day needs, only emergency needs and friendship.
>
> Out of the Cold has created a climate of genuine hands-on assistance to the vulnerable. The number of people exposed to the issues of poverty and homeless has increased. For the people who hosted the guests—they are beginning to be politicized. They are asking the question: Why poverty?

ISARC asks the same question: Why poverty? In its 1995 Poverty Profile, the National Council of Welfare concluded that:

> ...winning the war on poverty is not an unrealistic goal. Statistics Canada estimates that the cost of bringing all poor people out of poverty in 1995 would have been $16.3 billion. That's a huge, but not an outrageous amount of money in a country where the federal, provincial and territorial governments spent $339 billion in 1995, and where the value of all the goods and services produced was $776 billion.

A year later, in 1996—the year designated by the UN as the International Year for the Eradication of Poverty—more people were poor, and the incomes of the poor slipped even farther below the poverty line.

ISARC believes that defeating poverty is a matter of will. We can find the

resources if we decide we must. We seem to be able to identify resources for tax cuts which mainly benefit those with higher incomes.

The faith communities involved in our coalition have developed a response in the context of a framework for justice. ISARC realizes that it is not enough simply to call on governments to spend more money. There needs to be a framework to guide investments in the well-being of Canadian society as a whole. We propose the following Framework for Justice:

A Framework for Justice

1. Commitment to Jobs: A job strategy is the keystone of any social welfare system. The task is to support the creation of productive middle-income jobs. When more people are working, spending, and paying taxes, there is less pressure on the social safety net and adequate social policies become more affordable. There are both social and fiscal benefits to a high employment rate: for example, a healthier population and lower health care costs; less crime, violence and abuse and lower costs in the justice and social services systems.

2. Commitment to Income Security: If suitable employment opportunities are absent, alternate forms of income are essential. In Canada, they include Employment Insurance (EI) and welfare benefits. Eligibility requirements have been tightened up for EI. Because it is harder to get, more people must apply for welfare. But welfare is harder to get now too. Where is the security if the last resort program is not available to some people?

3. Commitment to Meeting Basic Needs: Social and economic policy proposals must be evaluated chiefly in terms of how they assist Canadians to meet basic life needs: food, shelter, clothing. Universal social entitlements, coupled with a progressive tax system, offer the simplest, cheapest, and least demeaning method to do that. This approach also tends to bind people together.

4. Commitment to Social and Economic Justice for Women and Children: Canadian women continue to live a far more precarious economic existence than do Canadian men. Women are more likely than men to live in poverty, particularly as single parents, or as seniors. In paid work, women face a persistent wage gap and are poorly represented in many well-paid occupations. Women still perform the majority of unpaid work in the household and community.

5. Commitment to Sustainability: Foundational issues of global and biospheric sustainability need to play a role in the making of social policy. The catastrophe of the East Coast fishery must inform our way of thinking about the care required in fisheries, agriculture, forestry, energy use, mining. Given the challenges of sustainability, the future of the social welfare state cannot be predicated on expectations of an ever-increasing gross domestic product (GDP).

6. Commitment to Fairness: When large segments of the population are made to pay the costs of fiscal policies, we live in a culture of injustice. A commitment by government to narrow the gap between the highest and lowest paid members of our workforce would overcome the polarizing tendencies that are dividing our society into rich and poor, educated and uneducated, and are shrinking our middle class. We must meet the needs of all before the wants of any. In addition, a tax system that redistributes wealth through progressive tax rates is essential to achieving equity and fairness.

In response to the voices of our neighbours, the Interfaith Social Assistance Reform Coalition is calling on governments, both federal and provincial, to recognize society's obligations to all our citizens by making the elimination of hunger, homelessness and poverty a priority for public policy. Governments have a moral responsibility which they cannot and must not abandon.

We urge our governments to develop a formal Social Charter consistent with the international standards and responsibilities to which Canada has committed itself i.e. the rights affirmed in the International Covenant on Economic, Social and Cultural Rights, to which Canada is a signatory. These rights include:

- the inherent dignity of the human person;
- the right of everyone to an adequate standard of living, including adequate food, clothing, and housing;
- the right of everyone to work and gain a living by work of one's own choosing;
- the right to enjoy the highest attainable physical and mental health; and
- the right to education.

We urge our governments, both federal and provincial, to take the specific measures necessary to live up to these international standards and to move people on social assistance and the working poor towards income adequacy.

Spending money without careful thought will not resolve the problems that people living on low incomes spoke of at the hearings. They called for jobs, quality child-care, access to education and training, and affordable housing as well as stronger income support programs. Imaginative, well-thought-out initiatives in each of these areas could do much to alleviate the poverty that is pressing more and more on individuals and on Canadian society as a whole.

ISARC urges governments to examine existing public policies to determine how to achieve the following:

- increase income security to adequate levels
- decrease dependency on food banks
- decrease the need for emergency shelters
- support community-based initiatives and programs
- make taxation fairer and more progressive, based upon the ability to pay
- support an increase in the supply and improved access to middle-income jobs
- improve the supply and access to support services such as child care
- hold governments accountable for their social responsibilities.

Through the vehicle of the Neighbour to Neighbour hearings, and in consultation with the faith and community groups who participated in this project, ISARC has developed detailed recommendations to begin to break the cycle of poverty and the debilitating hardship that it can cause to our neighbours. Those recommendations are included in the Resources section that follows this chapter.

The Resources section also includes the full texts of the International Covenant on Economic, Social and Cultural Rights and the Universal Declaration of Human Rights.

To enable citizens to track how we are doing in meeting our social priorities, we urge governments to provide an annual "social forecast" and to conduct a "social audit" on progress made from year to year. We are regularly inundated with financial information—on public sector budget-cutting, on the ups and downs of the stock market, on inflation, for example—but there is very little information given to the public on the social health of our community.

There is growing evidence that social health and community cohesion contribute to the success of regional and national economies and the vibrancy of our democratic form of government. We would do well to stop treating the social health of society as secondary to the demands of the market economy.

Finally, ISARC addresses an Open Letter to Faith Communities in Ontario.

Concerning Our Faith Communities

We, as the Interfaith Social Assistance Reform Coalition (ISARC)—representatives from the faith communities in Ontario, need to also address ourselves and remind our communities that the voices of our neighbours also speak to us. We

do not have the resources nor the responsibilities of government to provide econom-ic assistance and social programs that address the needs of citizens who are facing poverty and disability.

Yet we have been called as people of faith by our leaders and prophets:

- to work for the good of the larger community,
- to do acts of charity and compassion,
- to seek and do justice,
- to be in solidarity with the poor and vulnerable, and
- to remember the dignity of all human beings.

And we have responded by creating and funding community services, assisting individuals and families in crisis, calling for justice and compassion, remembering in prayer those who have been broken and disenfranchised, and showing love in numer-ous ways throughout this province. We have brought life and hope to many in our communities and found ways to treat each person as a neighbour.

The *Neighbour to Neighbour* hearing process would not have occurred if there were not many people of faith working among the poor in our cities and towns. The testi-monies tell of many ways in which congregations are working for community better-ment and are walking alongside or assisting those who need emergency assistance; need housing, food, counselling, and support care; need advocates; and need better housing and health care. The faith community is filling many gaps in service in this province; but our role is not to take the place of government services, housing pro-grams, disability pensions, and financial assistance. Therefore, many workers from faith communities are speaking out with the poor and decrying the abandonment of the poor and disabled in our province.

This is our predicament during these times. Often we have kept silent when we should have spoken. We have been satisfied with works of charity and not called for just solutions. Our monies and resources have sometimes helped to perpetuate pover-ty, rather than been being used to break the cycles of poverty, injustice, chaos, and spiritual degradation. We frequently have accepted the social class, race, gender, and economic barriers in our community. We unconsciously have worried about self-preservation, rather than opening our lives, congregations, and resources for the com-munity's betterment. At times, we have neglected the poor and disenfranchised who are members of our congregations.

It is time to reflect, repent, and renew ourselves and our congregations. It is time to sense solidarity with the poor and disabled. We need to go back to many of our scriptures and religious teachings which call us to remember the orphan, widow, stranger, prisoner, and disabled in the community. Can we create a new solidarity with them? We live in the same community/province. Can we listen to their voices and hold ourselves accountable?

As members of ISARC, we call each other and our faith communities to listen to the stories in this report and to respond out of compassion, justice, and love!

Resources

I. Detailed Recommendations from the Neighbour to Neighbour Process

1. General

1.1. That the federal and provincial governments recognize their social obligation by making the elimination of hunger, homelessness, and poverty a priority for public policy.

1.2 That the federal and provincial governments work to articulate these social obligations in a formal Social Charter for Canada consistent with the international standards rights and responsibilities to which Canada has obligated itself.

1.3 To respond to this public policy priority, that the Ontario Provincial Treasurer provide specific measures that will move those on assistance and the working poor toward income adequacy.

1.4 That the Provincial Government table in the Legislature a "Social Forecast" specifying the social objectives and consequences of social and fiscal policy decisions and that an annual Social Audit be provided on progress in the Legislature.

1.5 That the Provincial Government work with the federal and other provincial governments to establish substantial standards and effective enforcement mechanisms that hold governments accountable to addressing these needs and reflect the expressed goals of the international agreements to which we have pledged ourselves (Particularly Article 11 of the UN International Covenant on Economic, Social and Cultural Rights).

1.6 That the provincial government ensure basic rights to freedom of association, to appeal decisions, and to protections for all Ontarians under Health, Labour and Safety regulations and laws.

2. Income Support Systems

2.1 That an independent review be undertaken of federal and provincial social welfare legislation to ensure a commitment to basic principles—human dignity, mutual responsibility, social equity, economic equity, fiscal fairness—and that existing regulations comply.

2.2 That the Government of Ontario ensure all people have non-discriminatory access to support in times of crisis.

2.3 Ensure that income support programs are truly adequate to the real costs of living.

2.4 That the income supports programs and social services such as day care be adequate and expanded to include low wage earners.

2.5 That workfare programs be strictly voluntary for social assistance recipients, community organizations, and municipalities and that participants are covered by all employment, health and safety legislation.

2.6 That the Government of Ontario ensure that people leaving Addiction Rehabilitation Centres have immediate access to transitional funding adequate to the cost of living while they re-establish themselves in the community, as well as funding for training and education for those who need it.

2.7 That the Government of Ontario ensure that in all legislation and regulations, an accessible right to appeal decisions be maintained for participants. Benefits should be maintained during the appeal process and punitive action should not be taken for errors made by government administration of programs.

3. Work and Employment

3.1 That the Federal and Provincial Governments in Canada pursue a full employment and quality jobs policy giving serious consideration to the recommendations contained in the Alternative Federal Budget processes.

3.2 That the government looks at creative ways for creating paid employment that includes appropriate training particularly in the social and voluntary sector.

3.3 That Workfare be a voluntary program with additional resources for child care and participation.

3.4 That the Provincial Auditor be given a mandate to undertake a thorough analysis of the adequacy of programs to meets the needs of low-income individual and families, specifically auditing Workfare and providing the reason for those who have been removed from social assistance.

3.5 That the government makes a commitment to table in the Legislature estimates of how many participants will move to full-time employment and report annually on the effectiveness of these programs.

3.6 That new employment opportunities for young people (ages 18-35) be given specific attention.

3.7 That the Government of Ontario move to raise the minimum wage to reflect the cost of living for families with dependents

3.8 That the Provincial Government encourage and support community economic development projects and programs, including worker-owned co-ops, as a means of employment creation.

3.9 That the Provincial Government take measures to provide incentives for employers to hire new workers by:
i) reducing the standard work week without reducing wages.
ii) creating disincentives for overtime, such as the premium paid for overtime work, or collecting extra payroll taxes on overtime worked.
iii) offering tax subsidies to firms who reduce working hours and thus increase the number of workers employed.

3.10 That the Provincial Government encourage the Federal Government to remove ceilings for Canada Pension and Employment Insurance deductions for high wage earners, thus removing an incentive to do the same amount of work. Deductions per hour could be reduced, thus maintaining a consistent level of contributions to each fund.

4. Housing
4.1 That the Provincial Government provide financial resources and undertake programs to stimulate not-for-profit social housing initiatives across Ontario in the following ways: creating new housing and by providing a rent supplement program directed toward all low income people.

4.2 That the Provincial Government develop ways to ensure cooperation and collaboration by all stakeholders (tenants, landlords, community organizations) to ensure safe, affordable and accessible accommodation through joint public–private sector initiatives.

4.3 That the Provincial Government increase the shelter component for those on government assistance.

4.4 Increase the availability of emergency housing for persons (Age 16-70 years).

5. Health Care/Mental Health

5.1 That the principles in the Canada Health Act be strengthened and strictly enforced to ensure the future of our publicly funded and universal health care system in Ontario and in Canada.

5.2 That an adequate program of dental care be provided for all low-income people.

5.3 That the provincial Government recognize the importance of maintaining a mental health sector, that it not move to combine it with the general health sector, that funding be directed specifically to mental health issues; and that community and mental health resources be strengthened.

5.4 That the Provincial Government ensure accessible and affordable counselling services particularly for those with mental illnesses.

5.5 That the Provincial Government develop a housing policy (including rent-geared-to-income and supportive housing) for those suffering from mental illnesses such as schizophrenia.

5.6 That the Provincial Government develop a Long-Term Care Policy specific to the needs of those with serious mental illnesses.

5.7 That the user fees be dropped for those on low incomes and that the Government of Ontario reintroduce the drug buffer zone for the working poor.

5.8 That the Provincial Government work with the Federal Government to develop a national pharmacare policy that is supportive of those with any type of serious mental illness, particularly those with schizophrenia.

6. Supports to Community Participation

6.1 That as a support to employment and community participation, the Government of Ontario substantially expand the number of child care spaces in the province.

6.2 That the contribution and needs of parents with school age children—particularly single parents—be recognized and that programs and services be designed appropriately (e.g., no compulsory participation in workfare).

6.3 That the Provincial Government increases its support for literacy programs and adult access to secondary level education.

6.4 That the Government of Ontario develop specific measures for adequate funding to ensure accessibility to post-secondary education particularly for those on low incomes, in transition from welfare, and those with dependents.

6.5 That the Federal and Provincial Government reintroduce community–based alternatives to incarceration and transitional programs for re-entry into the community.

6.6 That the Provincial Government restore adequate funding for many community support services that have been eliminated and/or reduced (e.g., prevention work with youth, family violence programs with abusive men).

7. Aboriginal Peoples

7.1 That the Province of Ontario should support the aspirations of Aboriginal Peoples for control and self-determination in the design and delivery of social programs.

7.2 That the Provincial Government develop a comprehensive response to the recommendations of the Report of the Royal Commission on Aboriginal Peoples (RCAP) for discussion with the leaders and elders of First Nations and encourage broader public discussion of the RCAP recommendations.

8. Role of Government and Taxation

8.1 That the Provincial Government encourage the Federal Government in the development of standards for social programs that ensure of Canadian compliance with the international commitments Canada has made as a voluntary signator to human rights agreements, covenants, and declarations.

8.2 That the Provincial and Federal Government introduce an equitable progressive tax system based upon the ability to contribute and develop new and innovative approaches to taxation (e.g. taxation in currency speculation etc.).

8.3 That the Provincial Government immediately introduce a fair tax structure that adequately funds social programs and eliminates the social deficit in Ontario.

8.4 That the Provincial Government help ensure the adequate funding and public administration of social assistance and support services.

8.5 That the Provincial Government not proceed with the wholesale downloading to municipalities of responsibility for social services.

II. The Universal Declaration of Human Rights

Adopted and proclaimed by the United Nations General Assembly resolution 217 A (III) of 10, December 1948.

Preamble

Whereas recognition of the inherent dignity and of the equal and inalienable rights of all members of the human family is the foundation of freedom, justice and peace in the world,

Whereas disregard and contempt for human rights have resulted in barbarous acts which have outraged the conscience of mankind, and the advent of a world in which human beings shall enjoy freedom of speech and belief and freedom from fear and want has been proclaimed as the highest aspiration of the common people,

Whereas it is essential, if man is not to be compelled to have recourse, as a last resort, to rebellion against tyranny and oppression, that human rights should be protected by the rule of law,

Whereas it is essential to promote the development of friendly relations between nations,

Whereas the peoples of the United Nations have in the Charter reaffirmed their faith in fundamental human rights, in the dignity and worth of the human person and in the equal rights of men and women and have determined to promote social progress and better standards of life in larger freedom,

Whereas Member States have pledged themselves to achieve, in cooperation with the United Nations, the promotion of universal respect for and observance of human rights and fundamental freedoms,

Whereas a common understanding of these rights and freedoms is of the greatest importance for the full realization of this pledge,

Now, therefore, The General Assembly, Proclaims this Universal Declaration of Human Rights as a common standard of achievement for all peoples and all nations, to the end that every individual and every organ of society, keeping this Declaration constantly in mind, shall strive by teaching and education to promote respect for these rights and freedoms and by progressive measures, national and international, to secure their universal and effective recognition and observance, both among the peoples of Member States themselves and among the peoples of territories under their jurisdiction.

Article 1
All human beings are born free and equal in dignity and rights. They are endowed with reason and conscience and should act towards one another in a spirit of brotherhood.

Article 2
Everyone is entitled to all the rights and freedoms set forth in this Declaration, without distinction of any kind, such as race, colour, sex, language, religion, political or other opinion, national or social origin, property, birth or other status. Furthermore, no distinction shall be made on the basis of the political, jurisdictional or international status of the country or territory to which a person belongs, whether it be independent, trust, non-self-governing or under any other limitation of sovereignty.

Article 3
Everyone has the right to life, liberty and security of person.

Article 4
No one shall be held in slavery or servitude; slavery and the slave trade shall be prohibited in all their forms.

Article 5
No one shall be subjected to torture or to cruel, inhuman or degrading treatment or punishment.

Article 6
Everyone has the right to recognition everywhere as a person before the law.

Article 7
All are equal before the law and are entitled without any discrimination to equal protection of the law. All are entitled to equal protection against any discrimination in violation of this Declaration and against any incitement to such discrimination.

Article 8
Everyone has the right to an effective remedy by the competent national tribunals for acts violating the fundamental rights granted him by the constitution or by law.

Article 9
No one shall be subjected to arbitrary arrest, detention or exile.

Article 10
Everyone is entitled in full equality to a fair and public hearing by an independent and impartial tribunal, in the determination of his rights and obligations and of any criminal charge against him.

Article 11
Everyone charged with a penal offence has the right to be presumed innocent until proved guilty according to law in a public trial at which he has had all the guarantees necessary for his defence. No one shall be held guilty of any penal offence on account of any act or omission which did not constitute a penal offence, under national or international law, at the time when it was committed. Nor shall a heavier penalty be imposed than the one that was applicable at the time the penal offence was committed.

Article 12
No one shall be subjected to arbitrary interference with his privacy, family, home or correspondence, nor to attacks upon his honour and reputation. Everyone has the right to the protection of the law against such interference or attacks.

Article 13
Everyone has the right to freedom of movement and residence within the borders of each State.Everyone has the right to leave any country, including his own, and to return to his country.

Article 14
Everyone has the right to seek and to enjoy in other countries asylum from persecution. This right may not be invoked in the case of prosecutions genuinely arising from non–political crimes or from acts contrary to the purposes and principles of the United Nations.

Article 15
Everyone has the right to a nationality. No one shall be arbitrarily deprived of his nationality nor denied the right to change his nationality.

Article 16
Men and women of full age, without any limitation due to race, nationality or religion, have the right to marry and to found a family. They are entitled to equal

rights as to marriage, during marriage and at its dissolution. Marriage shall be entered into only with the free and full consent of the intending spouses. The family is the natural and fundamental group unit of society and is entitled to protection by society and the State.

Article 17
Everyone has the right to own property alone as well as in association with others. No one shall be arbitrarily deprived of his property.

Article 18
Everyone has the right to freedom of thought, conscience and religion; this right includes freedom to change his religion or belief, and freedom, either alone or in community with others and in public or private, to manifest his religion or belief in teaching, practice, worship and observance.

Article 19
Everyone has the right to freedom of opinion and expression; this right includes freedom to hold opinions without interference and to seek, receive and impart information and ideas through any media and regardless of frontiers.

Article 20
Everyone has the right to freedom of peaceful assembly and association. No one may be compelled to belong to an association.

Article 21
Everyone has the right to take part in the government of his country, directly or through freely chosen representatives. Everyone has the right to equal access to public service in his country. The will of the people shall be the basis of the authority of government; this will shall be expressed in periodic and genuine elections which shall be by universal and equal suffrage and shall be held by secret vote or by equivalent free voting procedures.

Article 22
Everyone, as a member of society, has the right to social security and is entitled to realization, through national effort and international co-operation and in accordance with the organization and resources of each State, of the economic, social and cultural rights indispensable for his dignity and the free development of his personality.

Article 23
Everyone has the right to work, to free choice of employment, to just and favour-

able conditions of work and to protection against unemployment. Everyone, without any discrimination, has the right to equal pay for equal work. Everyone who works has the right to just and favourable remuneration ensuring for himself and his family an existence worthy of human dignity, and supplemented, if necessary, by other means of social protection. Everyone has the right to form and to join trade unions for the protection of his interests.

Article 24
Everyone has the right to rest and leisure, including reasonable limitation of working hours and periodic holidays with pay.

Article 25
Everyone has the right to a standard of living adequate for the health and well-being of himself and of his family, including food, clothing, housing and medical care and necessary social services, and the right to security in the event of unemployment, sickness, disability, widowhood, old age or other lack of livelihood in circumstances beyond his control. Motherhood and childhood are entitled to special care and assistance. All children, whether born in or out of wedlock, shall enjoy the same social protection.

Article 26
Everyone has the right to education. Education shall be free, at least in the elementary and fundamental stages. Elementary education shall be compulsory. Technical and professional education shall be made generally available and higher education shall be equally accessible to all on the basis of merit. Education shall be directed to the full development of the human personality and to the strengthening of respect for human rights and fundamental freedoms. It shall promote understanding, tolerance and friendship among all nations, racial or religious groups, and shall further the activities of the United Nations for the maintenance of peace. Parents have a prior right to choose the kind of education that shall be given to their children.

Article 27
Everyone has the right freely to participate in the cultural life of the community, to enjoy the arts and to share in scientific advancement and its benefits. Everyone has the right to the protection of the moral and material interests resulting from any scientific, literary or artistic production of which he is the author.

Article 28
Everyone is entitled to a social and international order in which the rights and freedoms set forth in this Declaration can be fully realized.

Article 29

Everyone has duties to the community in which alone the free and full development of his personality is possible. In the exercise of his rights and freedoms, everyone shall be subject only to such limitations as are determined by law solely for the purpose of securing due recognition and respect for the rights and freedoms of others and of meeting the just requirements of morality, public order and the general welfare in a democratic society. These rights and freedoms may in no case be exercised contrary to the purposes and principles of the United Nations.

Article 30

Nothing in this Declaration may be interpreted as implying for any State, group or person any right to engage in any activity or to perform any act aimed at the destruction of any of the rights and freedoms set forth herein.

© 1997
Office of the United Nations High Commissioner for Human Rights
Geneva, Switzerland

III. The International Covenant on Economic, Social and Cultural Rights

Adopted and opened for signature, ratification and accession by the United Nations General Assembly resolution 2200A (XXI) of 16 December 1966, entry into force 3 January 1976, in accordance with article 27 status of ratifications.

Preamble

The States Parties to the present Covenant,

Considering that, in accordance with the principles proclaimed in the Charter of the United Nations, recognition of the inherent dignity and of the equal and inalienable rights of all members of the human family is the foundation of freedom, justice and peace in the world,

Recognizing that these rights derive from the inherent dignity of the human person,

Recognizing that, in accordance with the Universal Declaration of Human Rights, the ideal of free human beings enjoying freedom from fear and want can only be achieved if conditions are created whereby everyone may enjoy his economic, social and cultural rights, as well as his civil and political rights,

Considering the obligation of States under the Charter of the United Nations to promote universal respect for, and observance of, human rights and freedoms,

Realizing that the individual, having duties to other individuals and to the community to which he belongs, is under a responsibility to strive for the promotion and observance of the rights recognized in the present Covenant,

Agree upon the following articles:

PART I
Article 1

1. All peoples have the right of self-determination. By virtue of that right they freely determine their political status and freely pursue their economic, social and cultural development.

2. All peoples may, for their own ends, freely dispose of their natural wealth and resources without prejudice to any obligations arising out of international economic

co–operation, based upon the principle of mutual benefit, and international law. In no case may a people be deprived of its own means of subsistence.

3. The States Parties to the present Covenant, including those having responsibility for the administration of Non-Self-Governing and Trust Territories, shall promote the realization of the right of self-determination, and shall respect that right, in conformity with the provisions of the Charter of the United Nations.

PART II
Article 2
1. Each State Party to the present Covenant undertakes to take steps, individually and through international assistance and co-operation, especially economic and technical, to the maximum of its available resources, with a view to achieving progressively the full realization of the rights recognized in the present Covenant by all appropriate means, including particularly the adoption of legislative measures.

2. The States Parties to the present Covenant undertake to guarantee that the rights enunciated in the present Covenant will be exercised without discrimination of any kind as to race, colour, sex, language, religion, political or other opinion, national or social origin, property, birth or other status.

3. Developing countries, with due regard to human rights and their national economy, may determine to what extent they would guarantee the economic rights recognized in the present Covenant to non-nationals.

Article 3
The States Parties to the present Covenant undertake to ensure the equal right of men and women to the enjoyment of all economic, social and cultural rights set forth in the present Covenant.

Article 4
The States Parties to the present Covenant recognize that, in the enjoyment of those rights provided by the State in conformity with the present Covenant, the State may subject such rights only to such limitations as are determined by law only in so far as this may be compatible with the nature of these rights and solely for the purpose of promoting the general welfare in a democratic society.

Article 5
1. Nothing in the present Covenant may be interpreted as implying for any State, group or person any right to engage in any activity or to perform any act aimed at

the destruction of any of the rights or freedoms recognized herein, or at their limitation to a greater extent than is provided for in the present Covenant.

2. No restriction upon or derogation from any of the fundamental human rights recognized or existing in any country in virtue of law, conventions, regulations or custom shall be admitted on the pretext that the present Covenant does not recognize such rights or that it recognizes them to a lesser extent.

PART III
Article 6

1. The States Parties to the present Covenant recognize the right to work, which includes the right of everyone to the opportunity to gain his living by work which he freely chooses or accepts, and will take appropriate steps to safeguard this right.

2. The steps to be taken by a State Party to the present Covenant to achieve the full realization of this right shall include technical and vocational guidance and training programmes, policies and techniques to achieve steady economic, social and cultural development and full and productive employment under conditions safeguarding fundamental political and economic freedoms to the individual.

Article 7

The States Parties to the present Covenant recognize the right of everyone to the enjoyment of just and favourable conditions of work which ensure, in particular: (a) Remuneration which provides all workers, as a minimum, with: (i) Fair wages and equal remuneration for work of equal value without distinction of any kind, in particular women being guaranteed conditions of work not inferior to those enjoyed by men, with equal pay for equal work; (ii) A decent living for themselves and their families in accordance with the provisions of the present Covenant; (b) Safe and healthy working conditions; (c) Equal opportunity for everyone to be promoted in his employment to an appropriate higher level, subject to no considerations other than those of seniority and competence; (d) Rest, leisure and reasonable limitation of working hours and periodic holidays with pay, as well as remuneration for public holidays

Article 8

1. The States Parties to the present Covenant undertake to ensure: (a) The right of everyone to form trade unions and join the trade union of his choice, subject only to the rules of the organization concerned, for the promotion and protection of his economic and social interests. No restrictions may be placed on the exercise of this right other than those prescribed by law and which are necessary in a democratic society in the interests of national security or public order or for the protection of

the rights and freedoms of others; (b) The right of trade unions to establish national federations or confederations and the right of the latter to form or join international trade-union organizations; (c) The right of trade unions to function freely subject to no limitations other than those prescribed by law and which are necessary in a democratic society in the interests of national security or public order or for the protection of the rights and freedoms of others; (d) The right to strike, provided that it is exercised in conformity with the laws of the particular country.

2. This article shall not prevent the imposition of lawful restrictions on the exercise of these rights by members of the armed forces or of the police or of the administration of the State.

3. Nothing in this article shall authorize States Parties to the International Labour Organisation Convention of 1948 concerning Freedom of Association and Protection of the Right to Organize to take legislative measures which would prejudice, or apply the law in such a manner as would prejudice, the guarantees provided for in that Convention.

Article 9
The States Parties to the present Covenant recognize the right of everyone to social security, including social insurance.

Article 10
The States Parties to the present Covenant recognize that:

1. The widest possible protection and assistance should be accorded to the family, which is the natural and fundamental group unit of society, particularly for its establishment and while it is responsible for the care and education of dependent children. Marriage must be entered into with the free consent of the intending spouses.

2. Special protection should be accorded to mothers during a reasonable period before and after childbirth. During such period working mothers should be accorded paid leave or leave with adequate social security benefits.

3. Special measures of protection and assistance should be taken on behalf of all children and young persons without any discrimination for reasons of parentage or other conditions. Children and young persons should be protected from economic and social exploitation. Their employment in work harmful to their morals or health or dangerous to life or likely to hamper their normal development should be

punishable by law. States should also set age limits below which the paid employment of child labour should be prohibited and punishable by law.

Article 11

1. The States Parties to the present Covenant recognize the right of everyone to an adequate standard of living for himself and his family, including adequate food, clothing and housing, and to the continuous improvement of living conditions. The States Parties will take appropriate steps to ensure the realization of this right, recognizing to this effect the essential importance of international co-operation based on free consent.

2. The States Parties to the present Covenant, recognizing the fundamental right of everyone to be free from hunger, shall take, individually and through international co-operation, the measures, including specific programmes, which are needed: (a) To improve methods of production, conservation and distribution of food by making full use of technical and scientific knowledge, by disseminating knowledge of the principles of nutrition and by developing or reforming agrarian systems in such a way as to achieve the most efficient development and utilization of natural resources; (b) Taking into account the problems of both food-importing and food-exporting countries, to ensure an equitable distribution of world food supplies in relation to need.

Article 12

1. The States Parties to the present Covenant recognize the right of everyone to the enjoyment of the highest attainable standard of physical and mental health.

2. The steps to be taken by the States Parties to the present Covenant to achieve the full realization of this right shall include those necessary for: (a) The provision for the reduction of the stillbirth-rate and of infant mortality and for the healthy development of the child; (b) The improvement of all aspects of environmental and industrial hygiene; (c) The prevention, treatment and control of epidemic, endemic, occupational and other diseases; (d) The creation of conditions which would assure to all medical serviceand medical attention in the event of sickness.

Article 13

1. The States Parties to the present Covenant recognize the right of everyone to education. They agree that education shall be directed to the full development of the human personality and the sense of its dignity, and shall strengthen the respect for human rights and fundamental freedoms. They further agree that education shall enable all persons to participate effectively in a free society, promote understanding, tolerance and friendship among all nations and all racial, ethnic or reli-

gious groups, and further the activities of the United Nations for the maintenance of peace.

2. The States Parties to the present Covenant recognize that, with a view to achieving the full realization of this right: (a) Primary education shall be compulsory and available free to all; (b) Secondary education in its different forms, including technical and vocational secondary education, shall be made generally available and accessible to all by every appropriate means, and in particular by the progressive introduction of free education; (c) Higher education shall be made equally accessible to all, on the basis of capacity, by every appropriate means, and in particular by the progressive introduction of free education; (d) Fundamental education shall be encouraged or intensified as far as possible for those persons who have not received or completed the whole period of their primary education; (e) The development of a system of schools at all levels shall be actively pursued, an adequate fellowship system shall be established, and the material conditions of teaching staff shall be continuously improved.

3. The States Parties to the present Covenant undertake to have respect for the liberty of parents and, when applicable, legal guardians to choose for their children schools, other than those established by the public authorities, which conform to such minimum educational standards as may be laid down or approved by the State and to ensure the religious and moral education of their children in conformity with their own convictions.

4. No part of this article shall be construed so as to interfere with the liberty of individuals and bodies to establish and direct educational institutions, subject always to the observance of the principles set forth in paragraph I of this article and to the requirement that the education given in such institutions shall conform to such minimum standards as may be laid down by the State.

Article 14

Each State Party to the present Covenant which, at the time of becoming a Party, has not been able to secure in its metropolitan territory or other territories under its jurisdiction compulsory primary education, free of charge, undertakes, within two years, to work out and adopt a detailed plan of action for the progressive implementation, within a reasonable number of years, to be fixed in the plan, of the principle of compulsory education free of charge for all.

Article 15

1. The States Parties to the present Covenant recognize the right of everyone: (a)

To take part in cultural life; (b) To enjoy the benefits of scientific progress and its applications; (c) To benefit from the protection of the moral and material interests resulting from any scientific, literary or artistic production of which he is the author.

2. The steps to be taken by the States Parties to the present Covenant to achieve the full realization of this right shall include those necessary for the conservation, the development and the diffusion of science and culture.

3. The States Parties to the present Covenant undertake to respect the freedom indispensable for scientific research and creative activity.

4. The States Parties to the present Covenant recognize the benefits to be derived from the encouragement and development of international contacts and co-operation in the scientific and cultural fields.

PART IV
Article 16

1. The States Parties to the present Covenant undertake to submit in conformity with this part of the Covenant reports on the measures which they have adopted and the progress made in achieving the observance of the rights recognized herein.

2. (a) All reports shall be submitted to the Secretary-General of the United Nations, who shall transmit copies to the Economic and Social Council for consideration in accordance with the provisions of the present Covenant; (b) The Secretary-General of the United Nations shall also transmit to the specialized agencies copies of the reports, or any relevant parts therefrom, from States Parties to the present Covenant which are also members of these specialized agencies in so far as these reports, or parts therefrom, relate to any matters which fall within the responsibilities of the said agencies in accordance with their constitutional instruments.

Article 17

1. The States Parties to the present Covenant shall furnish their reports in stages, in accordance with a programme to be established by the Economic and Social Council within one year of the entry into force of the present Covenant after consultation with the States Parties and the specialized agencies concerned.

2. Reports may indicate factors and difficulties affecting the degree of fulfilment of obligations under the present Covenant.

3. Where relevant information has previously been furnished to the United Nations or to any specialized agency by any State Party to the present Covenant, it will not be necessary to reproduce that information, but a precise reference to the information so furnished will suffice.

Article 18
Pursuant to its responsibilities under the Charter of the United Nations in the field of human rights and fundamental freedoms, the Economic and Social Council may make arrangements with the specialized agencies in respect of their reporting to it on the progress made in achieving the observance of the provisions of the present Covenant falling within the scope of their activities. These reports may include particulars of decisions and recommendations on such implementation adopted by their competent organs.

Article 19
The Economic and Social Council may transmit to the Commission on Human Rights for study and general recommendation or, as appropriate, for information the reports concerning human rights submitted by States in accordance with articles 16 and 17, and those concerning human rights submitted by the specialized agencies in accordance with article 18.

Article 20
The States Parties to the present Covenant and the specialized agencies concerned may submit comments to the Economic and Social Council on any general recommendation under article 19 or reference to such general recommendation in any report of the Commission on Human Rights or any documentation referred to therein.

Article 21
The Economic and Social Council may submit from time to time to the General Assembly reports with recommendations of a general nature and a summary of the information received from the States Parties to the present Covenant and the specialized agencies on the measures taken and the progress made in achieving general observance of the rights recognized in the present Covenant.

Article 22
The Economic and Social Council may bring to the attention of other organs of the United Nations, their subsidiary organs and specialized agencies concerned with furnishing technical assistance any matters arising out of the reports referred to in this part of the present Covenant which may assist such bodies in deciding, each within its field of competence, on the advisability of international measures likely

to contribute to the effective progressive implementation of the present Covenant.

Article 23

The States Parties to the present Covenant agree that international action for the achievement of the rights recognized in the present Covenant includes such methods as the conclusion of conventions, the adoption of recommendations, the furnishing of technical assistance and the holding of regional meetings and technical meetings for the purpose of consultation and study organized in conjunction with the Governments concerned.

Article 24

Nothing in the present Covenant shall be interpreted as impairing the provisions of the Charter of the United Nations and of the constitutions of the specialized agencies which define the respective responsibilities of the various organs of the United Nations and of the specialized agencies in regard to the matters dealt with in the present Covenant.

Article 25

Nothing in the present Covenant shall be interpreted as impairing the inherent right of all peoples to enjoy and utilize fully and freely their natural wealth and resources.

PART V
Article 26

1. The present Covenant is open for signature by any State Member of the United Nations or member of any of its specialized agencies, by any State Party to the Statute of the International Court of Justice, and by any other State which has been invited by the General Assembly of the United Nations to become a party to the present Covenant.

2. The present Covenant is subject to ratification. Instruments of ratification shall be deposited with the Secretary–General of the United Nations.

3. The present Covenant shall be open to accession by any State referred to in paragraph 1 of this article.

4. Accession shall be effected by the deposit of an instrument of accession with the Secretary-General of the United Nations.
5. The Secretary-General of the United Nations shall inform all States which have signed the present Covenant or acceded to it of the deposit of each instrument of ratification or accession.

Article 27

1. The present Covenant shall enter into force three months after the date of the deposit with the Secretary-General of the United Nations of the thirty-fifth instrument of ratification or instrument of accession.

2. For each State ratifying the present Covenant or acceding to it after the deposit of the thirty–fifth instrument of ratification or instrument of accession, the present Covenant shall enter into force three months after the date of the deposit of its own instrument of ratification or instrument of accession.

Article 28

The provisions of the present Covenant shall extend to all parts of federal States without any limitations or exceptions.

Article 29

1. Any State Party to the present Covenant may propose an amendment and file it with the Secretary-General of the United Nations. The Secretary-General shall thereupon communicate any proposed amendments to the States Parties to the present Covenant with a request that they notify him whether they favour a conference of States Parties for the purpose of considering and voting upon the proposals. In the event that at least one third of the States Parties favours such a conference, the Secretary–General shall convene the conference under the auspices of the United Nations. Any amendment adopted by a majority of the States Parties present and voting at the conference shall be submitted to the General Assembly of the United Nations for approval.

2. Amendments shall come into force when they have been approved by the General Assembly of the United Nations and accepted by a two-thirds majority of the States Parties to the present Covenant in accordance with their respective constitutional processes.

3. When amendments come into force they shall be binding on those States Parties which have accepted them, other States Parties still being bound by the provisions of the present Covenant and any earlier amendment which they have accepted.

Article 30

Irrespective of the notifications made under article 26, paragraph 5, the Secretary-General of the United Nations shall inform all States referred to in paragraph I of the same article of the following particulars: (a) Signatures, ratifications and accessions under article 26; (b) The date of the entry into force of the present Covenant under article 27 and the date of the entry into force of any amendments under article 29.

Article 31

1. The present Covenant, of which the Chinese, English, French, Russian and Spanish texts are equally authentic, shall be deposited in the archives of the United Nations.

2. The Secretary-General of the United Nations shall transmit certified copies of the present Covenant to all States referred to in article 26.

© *1997*

Office of the United Nations High Commissioner for Human Rights Geneva, Switzerland

The Our Schools/Our Selves Series

James Lorimer & Company is now distributing and
marketing the Our Schools/Our Selves book series.

New titles will be published as series titles.

The backlist of titles is now available to the trade
through James Lorimer & Company.

Libraries and bookstores can order *Our Schools/Our Selves* Series titles
from James Lorimer and Company through its distributor:

Formac Distributing Limited
5502 Atlantic Street
Halifax B3H 1G4
Toll free order line 1-800-565-1975
Fax orders (902) 435-0166